AROUND THE TABLE WITH

Sandi Patty

faith, family, & food

Published by Stylos Records
www.stylosrecords.com
www.sandipatty.com

Contents

A Note from Sandi:

Dining. Food. Conversation. Laughter. Feast. Parties. Delicious. Holidays.   These are just a few of words that come to mind when I think of dining and cooking. One of the central themes in our home has always been the celebration of life through...yes food. But food and dining are more than just sitting and eating. It's an event. It's an experience. Often around the table, its been group therapy or comedy hour. A time to catch up the family on each other's events.

When the kids were little, we would make sure that we always had dinner together in between all the kids' activities. Believe me, that wasn't always easy to do as the kids had sports, music, dance, and other school activities. So we might gather around the table and have dinner at 3:45 in the afternoon or 8:00 in the evening.

One of the things that Don and I always prayed for was that the kids would feel comfortable talking to us. So even when they were little, we began what we call our "high/low" conversation. Everyone would go around the table and talk about what was good or "high" about the day and what was bad or "low" about the day. It gave everyone an opportunity to talk and more importantly everyone an opportunity to listen. Some days, especially when they were all little, the "high" might be that the school lunch was chicken and noodles and the "low" might be that they had to run 10 straight minutes in gym class.

But as they got older, the "high" became more substantial and the "lows" became more meaningful. It became a great way to begin conversation around the table.

For better or worse, food has been a big part of my story. As I'm reshaping my view on the importance of food in my own life, the "stories" that have been created because of gathering together around the table have become so much more important. There might be a few, shall we say, "indulgent" recipes that we still included. Everything in moderation, right? But, there are also some new recipes that we've adopted to help in my own weight-loss life change.

In the pages that follow you will find recipes, stories, pictures, funny sayings, conversation starters or perhaps meaningful moments that have been a central focus our of gatherings. This truly was a family project, with so many of our kids, my parents, Don's family and friends contributing recipes that we love. We pray that you and your family will find meaningful moments as you all gather around the table.

Jonathan

Erin

Donnie

Sam

Jenn

Sandi & Don

Collin & Anna

Mollie

Aly

This book is dedicated to my Grandma Grace Patty and my Grandma Mabel Tunnell
From donuts to spaghetti to peanut brittle they taught me about the experience of
cooking and sharing a meal with your family. You both would be so proud of this boo
as we are all so proud of having known you both.

Many thank you's to
so many for making this happen—

My amazing family who loves to cook, and I thank you sweet family for taking the time to put this project together.

Anna Trent - For doing so much that no one ever even sees.   I appreciate you so very much.   I couldn't do what I do without you.

Natalie Farmer - For always figuring out a way to make anything happen and for looking out for us in a way that only you know how.

Mike Atkins - For being such a champion of this project and so many more dreams to come.

Nicole Carpenter - what an eye you have for great photographs and details. You captured our family spirit through our photos.
Love to work with you girl.

Daniel McCarthy and Nic Carfa at Concept Culture - Thank you for being so willing to work on a project filled with many "firsts" for all of us. The cookbook is beautiful and you all are so great to work with.

Margo and Nell of M&N Catering - You all have been apart of so many family memories because of your cooking. You brought your expertise to this project. You tested and tasted everything and presented it in such a gorgeous way. How fitting for you two to be apart of this. We love you!

Gloria Gaither, Wade & Stephanie Carignan, Andrew Frank, Julie Short, Amy & Loz for Presh Homes - For all the details, for compiling the recipes, for jumping into a project that none of us have ever tackled before, for contributing and collaborating... Thank you!

Photography by:
www.elocineyephotography.com
www.cgindy.com

Art Direction and Design by:
www.conceptculture.com

Appetizers

Brie En Croute

Owner: Anna

Prep Time: 15 minutes

Servings: 12-16

Total Time: 1 hour and 15 minutes

. . . .

Ingredients:

1 sheet pre-packaged puff pastry
1 12-ounce brie cheese wheel
1/4 cup dried cranberries
3 tablespoon honey
3 teaspoon fresh rosemary, finely chopped
3 teaspoon fresh thyme, finely chopped
1 egg
1 tablespoon water
Crackers or hearty whole grain bread

. . . .

Directions:

Preheat oven to 350 degrees F. In small bowl, mix cranberries, honey, 2 teaspoons rosemary and 2 teaspoons thyme. Set aside. Roll out puff pastry on non-stick baking sheet. In middle of puff pastry, pour mixture into a circle. Cover immediately with brie cheese. Mix egg and water into small bowl to make an egg wash. With a pastry brush, coat the exposed edges of the puff pastry with the egg wash. Fold corners of puff pastry onto the top of the brie and fold in remaining puff pastry into center, covering the entire brie wheel. Turn over puff pastry, so the folds are on the bottom. (Optional: Roll out another sheet of puff pastry, and with cookie cutters cut out shapes to put on top.) Brush the top and sides of puff pastry with egg wash and dust with additional rosemary and thyme. Bake in the oven for 35-40 minutes, or until puff pastry is golden. Let cool for 30 minutes. Serve with crackers or slices of hearty whole grain bread.

For a healthier option, shave off the top rind of the brie. Bake for 10 minutes. Add half of honey mixture on top of brie. Bake for an additional 10 minutes. Eliminating the puff pastry saves a lot of fat calories and still creates a festive appetizer.

Buffalo Chicken Dip

Owner: Natalie (Sandi's Business Manager)
Servings: 8-10
Prep Time: 15 minutes
Total Time: 30 minutes

Ingredients:

2 whole rotisserie chickens
(or 5 cooked chicken breasts)
1 12-ounce bottle hot sauce
8 ounces cream cheese
1 16-ounce bottle prepared ranch dressing
2 cups shredded cheddar cheese

Directions

Remove white and dark meat from rotisserie chickens and chop into 1/2 inch pieces. Toss chicken with hot sauce until fully coated. Layer chicken mixture at the bottom of a 9x13 pan.

In separate bowl, beat cream cheese and ranch dressing until smooth. Pour cream cheese mixture on top of chicken mixture, then sprinkle the cheddar cheese on top.

Bake at 350 degrees for 20 minutes, or until cheese is bubbling. Serve with tortilla chips and celery.

Quick Quesadillas

Owner: Sandi
Servings: 1
Prep Time: 3 minutes
Total Time: 3 minutes 30 seconds

. . . .

Ingredients:

2 small flour tortillas
Spray butter
1/4 cup shredded cheddar/monetary jack cheese
Optional Ingredients:
Ground beef, grilled chicken, chorizo
Sliced onions, tomatoes, avocado

Directions:

Spray one tortilla with butter. Sprinkle cheese and fillings on tortilla. Top with second tortilla. Heat large pan on stove and use non-stick cooking spray on surface.
Place tortilla on pan for about 3-4 minutes on each side. Cut into triangles with a pizza cutter.

Story:

This might be the best after school snack. Easy and inexpensive! When the kids were ages 12 and under we made these by the dozen. And if you want the kids to help with this snack, and make the recipe really easy for you, put your quesadilla on a plate (instead of heating it on a pan) and heat it in the microwave. Easy!

Sweet-N-Sour Mini Wieners

Owner: Mike Patty (Sandi's Brother)
Servings: 10–12
Prep Time: 30 minutes
Total Time: 30 minutes

. . . .

Ingredients:

1 16-ounce package of small sausage links
1 cup barbeque sauce
1 cup grape jelly

Directions

In medium saucepan or slow cooker, combine all ingredients. Bring sauce to a boil, reduce heat and let simmer for 15 minutes. Serve as appetizer with toothpicks as the utensils.

Story:

3 ingredients. 7 high school open houses and counting. A must have on the come and go celebration menu. Whoever thought that 3 ingredients could be so good?

Black Bean & Corn Salsa

Owner: Collin
Servings: 4
Prep Time: 10 minutes
Total Time: 25 minutes

. . . .

Ingredients:

1 14 ounce can black beans, drained
1 14 ounce can sweet corn kernels, drained
1/2 cup red onion, diced
1/4 cup cilantro leaves, chopped
3 tbsp bacon, baked and finely chopped
1 tbsp sugar
3 tbsp white wine vinegar
Salt and pepper

Directions

Combine all ingredients in bowl. Season as desired. Chill for 15 minutes and serve with tortilla chips.

Ann's Tabouli

Owner: Ann Aluise (Don's Aunt)
Servings: 8
Prep Time: 15 minutes
Total Time: 20 minutes

. . . .

Ingredients:

2 bunches parsley
3/4 cup wheat
1 medium cucumber
1 small tomato, firm
2 bunches green onions
1/3 cup oil (half olive oil, half canola oil)
4 tablespoons lemon juice
Salt to taste

Directions:

Soak wheat in 2 cups water for 2 hours before mixing. Very finely chop the tomato, onions, parsley and cucumber. Add the oil, juice and salt. Mix well and serve.

Tip :

Use kitchen shears to chop the parsley. It's a lot easier than cutting the parsley.

Guacamole

Owner: Collin
Servings: 4
Prep Time: 15 minutes
Total Time: 15 minutes

Ingredients:

1 large avocado
1/4 cup red onion, diced
Salt, to taste (the avocado does need a lot of salt but taste as your adding it)
1/8 cup pineapple, finely diced
1 tablespoon pineapple juice
Juice from 1/2 lime
1/2 teaspoon cumin

Directions

Cut the avocado in half. (The core will come out on one side or the other.) Using a spoon, remove the core. Then, using the same spoon, remove the avocado from the skin, scooping it from the bottom. Cut into small pieces and place into bowl. Combine all remaining ingredients and mix. Be careful not to over mix, just make sure the ingredients are combined well.

Tip :

Guacamole can be used as more than just a dip. Use it as a spread on sandwiches or burgers. Use it as apart of a salad or put it in soups like chili or Mexican chicken soup.

Pepperoni Bread

Owner: Collin
Servings: 10-12 Slices

Ingredients:

1 can refrigerated French loaf dough
1 8-ounce package turkey pepperoni
2 cloves garlic, minced
3 tablespoons fresh basil, chopped
1-2 cups shredded Italian style cheese
(a blend of different Italian cheese is a
great package to use, such as mozzarella
or parmesan)
1 egg
2 tablespoons water
Salt and pepper to taste

Directions

Preheat oven to 375 degrees F. On a large
cookie sheet, roll out French loaf into a large
rectangle. On one long edge of the dough, place
cheese, pepperoni, garlic, basil, salt, and pepper.
Leaving about 2 inches of space on the edge, the
ingredients should cover about 3-4 inches. Starting
with the end of the loaf that has the ingredients,
start rolling the dough to create a long roll. In a
small bowl, wisk egg and water to create egg wash.
Using a pastry brush spread the egg wash over
the roll. Sprinkle with kosher salt and fresh cracked
pepper. Bake for 20-25 minutes, or until golden
brown. Slice into pieces and serve hot. (Although, I
always prefer cold leftovers of the bread.)

Salsa

Owner: Andrew (Aly's Boyfriend)
Servings: 8
Prep Time: 45 minutes
Total Time: 1 hour 30 minutes

Ingredients:

1 1/2 pounds of tomatoes
5 cloves of garlic
6 banana peppers
1/4 cup cilantro, chopped
1 small yellow onion, diced
1 hot chili pepper
Juice from 1/2 of a lime

Directions:

Roast half of the tomatoes and all of the banana peppers for 35 minutes at 400 degrees F. Remove from the oven and let cool. Chop roasted tomatoes. In a food processor, combine the tomatoes, garlic, banana peppers, cilantro, onion, chili and lime juice. Stop when the salsa has a thicker, soupier consistency. Serve with tortilla chips.

Texas Caviar

Owner: Sandi
Servings: 8
Prep Time: 10 minutes
Total Time: 10 minutes

Ingredients:

2 15-ounce cans black eye peas, drained
1 bell pepper, chopped
6 spring onions, finely chopped
8 ounces Italian dressing
Hot sauce to taste

Directions:

Mix ingredients and enjoy with corn chips of your choice. Easy and delicious!

Ann's Spinach Squares

Owner: Ann Aluise (Don's Aunt)
Servings: 9 small squares
Prep Time: 15 minutes
Total time: 40 minutes

. . . .

Ingredients:

2 cups cooked chopped spinach, drained
4 tablespoons flour
4 tablespoons butter
1 tablespoon minced onion
1 teaspoon salt
2 cups milk
1 cup grated American cheese
2 eggs lightly beaten
Hot sauce, 1-2 teaspoons or adjusted to taste

Directions

Preheat oven to 350 degrees F. Melt butter, add
onion and cook until tender. Add flour, and milk;
cook until thickens. Add cheese and stir. Add a dash
of hot sauce to the beaten eggs. Combine spinach,
stove mixture and egg mixture in 8x8 baking dish.
Bake for 30 minutes.

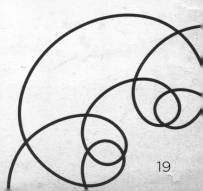

Papa's Popcorn

Owner: Papa (Ron Patty—Sandi's dad)
Servings: 4–5
Prep Time: 15 minutes
Total Time: 15 minutes

Ingredients:

1 cup popcorn
1/4 cup shortening (or vegetable oil)
1 pinch of garlic salt
1 tablespoon of regular salt
2 tablespoons of melted butter (or more,
depending on one's cravings)

Directions:

Put the shortening in thick bottom metal pan,
then the popcorn and garlic salt. Stir things
around so the kernels are submerged,
surrounded (baptized) in the oil. (Sounds
religious doesn't it?). Well, in our family,
popcorn is religious.) Continue to shake lightly as
the kernels pop. The shaking forces the
un-popped kernels to the bottom of the hot pan.
After the kernels have popped,
generously salt the popcorn (again, your taste is
the deciding factor), and then add the butter with
a tablespoon, sprinkling the melted butter over
the corn, stirring, then sprinkling, stirring, etc.

Tip :

I used to let the shortening get hot, hot, hot,
but I don't anymore. Your cooking surface
should be a little hotter than medium. Putting
the popcorn in just after the shortening
allows the shortening to soak into the kernels
for a time. That soaking in process makes the
kernels explode from the inside out. A thick
bottom metal pan is the best. The lid should
not fit airtight. There are even some electric
poppers with a domed clear plastic lid at
most local super stores that are perfect for
only $20. Never a bad batch.

Simple Grilled Bruschetta

Owner: Aly
Servings: 8–12
Prep Time: 5 minutes
Total Time: 10 minutes

Ingredients:

1 French baguette
4 cloves garlic
4 diced Roma tomatoes
1/4 cup fresh basil
Olive oil
Sea salt

Directions

Dice the tomatoes into small chunks and chop basil. Combine and toss with 1 to 2 tablespoons olive oil and sprinkle with sea salt. Set aside

Cut garlic cloves in half. Cut baguette into diagonal pieces. Spread with olive oil and grill 1 to 2 minutes until you have nice grill marks. Remove from grill and rub the garlic all over the pieces of bread. Spoon the tomato and basil mixture over the bread and enjoy!

Tip :

Rubbing whole pieces of garlic warm bread is an easy and quick way to spice up normal bread. The heat from the bread allows the flavor to spread into the bread. Think about rubbing garlic on bread, chicken, beef or fish as a way to infuse some garlic flavor in a new way.

Proscuitto Wraps

Owner: Anna
Servings: 16 pieces
Prep Time: 15 minutes
Total Time: 30 minutes

Ingredients:

6 slices prosciutto, thinly sliced
16 basil leaves
16 ounces fresh mozzarella, cut into 1 ounce portions (about 2 inch cubes)
Salt and pepper
16 toothpicks

Directions:

Season mozzarella cubes with salt and pepper. Slice each piece of prosciutto into 3 long slices. Wrap basil leaf around mozzarella cube. Wrap one slice of prosciutto around basil. Secure with 1 toothpick. Chill for 15 minutes and serve.

Story:

When our kids were little, (this seems to be a theme in this book—hey we were desperate for ideas) we would often create "grown up" meals that we could eat at home. This way the kids could learn how to act at a "grown up" event without actually having to cart all of our kids to a restaurant. One of our very favorites, to this day, is what we call Hors D'oeuvres Dinners. And the childhood classic was bologna wrapped with American cheese. We can do these now as real grown up hors d'oeuvres variations—
Water chestnuts with cooked bacon wrapped around it or mozzarella ball with prosciutto ham. Get creative in using different ingredients to create your wraps. You'd be surprised what you can create with just a few items.

— Sandi

Soups and Salads

Cucumber & Red Onion Salad

Owner: Anna
Servings: 6
Prep Time: 15 minutes
Total Time: 1 hour & 15 minutes

· ·

Ingredients:

1 large cucumber
3/4 cup red onion, cut into 3 inch slices
1/2 cup water
4 tablespoon apple cinder vinegar
1 tablespoon sugar
Salt and pepper to taste

Directions:

Slice cucumber down the middle lengthwise. Cut
cucumber into thin slices. Cut red onions into 3 inch
slices. Combine all ingredients into medium size bowl.
Cover and refrigerate for at least one hour.
Serve chilled.

Taco Soup or "Deer Creek Soup"

Owner: Sandi
Servings: 8
Prep Time: 8-10 minutes
Total Time: 5 hours in a slow cooker or 1 hour on the stove

. . . .

Ingredients:

1 can black beans
1 can dark red beans
1 can pinto beans
1 can navy beans
1 can great northern beans
1 can spicy diced tomato
1 package dry ranch dressing
Package of corn chips
Grated cheddar cheese

Directions:

Place all ingredients into a pan or slow cooker. Use the juice from the beans. No need to drain. Cook on stovetop for about one hour or until flavors blend (or cook in slow cooker for about 5 hours). Place corn chips in bottom of bowl. Top with soup. Top soup with cheese.

Story:

This recipe has so many names, but the one we have used is "Deer Creek Soup" because this is a soup that is served so often at the Deer Creek High School Football games. Deer Creek is the name of Sam's school.

- Sandi

Tip:

You can vary this a little by adding ground beef or ground sausage. Makes it delicious.

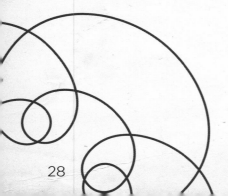

Mexican Chicken Soup

Owner: Anna & Collin
Servings: 6-8
Prep Time: 1 hour
Total Time: 1 hour & 30 minutes

Ingredients:

4 large chicken breasts
6 cups reduced sodium chicken stock
2 12-ounce cans of black beans
1 12-ounce can sweet corn kernels
1 8-ounce can of diced tomatoes with
Mexican spices
1 cup red onion, diced
1/2 cup cilantro leaves, chopped
1 2-ounce can of green chiles
2 cloves garlic, finely chopped
1/4 cup taco seasoning, add more to taste
2 tablespoons cumin
1 tablespoon paprika
Salt and pepper to taste
Sliced avocado (optional)
Shredded cheese (optional)

Directions:

Pour chicken stock in large pot and add chicken. Turn heat to high and bring to boil. Add taco seasoning. Boil chicken until thoroughly cooked and tender, about 30-40 minutes. Keep pot on heat, taking out chicken breasts and shredding the chicken. Put shredded chicken back into pot. Add all remaining ingredients. Let soup simmer an additional 30 minutes. Serve hot with sliced avocado and shredded cheese on top.

The most important thing for a soup: simmering it slowly. All the ingredients come together when they have time to live together in the pot for awhile. Continue to taste along the way and season it to your palate preference. Cumin is the secret ingredient in this recipe. And it's a favorite spice in our pantry that adds a subtle yet mysterious spice in a lot of our recipes.

Grown Up Grilled Cheese Sandwich

Owner: Aly
Servings: 4
Prep Time: 20 minutes
Total Time: 40 minutes

. . . .

Ingredients:

2 cups melting cheese (I occasionally even throw in a smoked cheese like gouda or cheddar)
1/2 stick unsalted butter
1 cup spinach
1/2 tsp cayenne pepper (more if you like it spicy)
1 tomato
8 slices bacon, cooked and broken into 2 pieces
8 slices freshly baked thick bread

Tip:

This is a recipe you can play with. I love grilled cheese and love it even more when there are little extras hidden inside. Change up the cheeses you include and use different kinds meat. Once you have the process down, you can change the ingredients to make great flavors.

Directions:

Together in a food processor; add the cheese, and butter. Pulse until combined, add the spinach and run the processor until the spinach is well incorporated. Add the cayenne pepper and give it another quick pulse.

Spread the cheese and spinach mixture onto 4 slices of the bread. Crumble the bacon and use two slices per sandwich. Add two slices of tomato. Top each sandwich with another piece of bread.

(If you have a Panini maker you will definitely want to take it out for this. If not you can simply use a skillet.)

Panini Maker:
Each model is different. Watch your sandwich to get to your perfect amount of golden crispiness

Skillet Method
Melt a tablespoon of butter in the pan at medium high heat. Add two sandwiches at a time. When sandwiches are in pan, place a heavy pot on top to get a good brown on the bread. Flip when your bread has a nice golden color - about 3 minutes.

Story:

Grilled cheese sandwiches have been a staple around our table. They are fast and good. Often when the kids were little and we would have "grown up" food, many times I would make grilled cheese. One of our kids, Erin, ate grilled cheese every single day. We took a cruise tour one summer to Greece and Erin ordered grilled cheese. The waiter ended up bringing her something hot wrapped in foil. When she opened it, it was little a slab of cheese they had grilled on the grill. No bread, no nothing. Simply "grilled cheese." We had a good laugh over this one.

One day at our home, I was trying my best to multitask. I was doing an interview, trying to fold the last load of laundry before I left on tour, and fixing a quick lunch for one of the kids who needed to go to dance class. I made grilled cheese for Jenn and handed it to her without really paying much attention. In a few seconds I saw her having a hard time breathing and she was leaning over the sink in the kitchen. I quickly ran over to her as she pulled something out of her mouth. Apparently in my haste to multitask, I had left the plastic ON the cheese. Not a good idea.

- Sandi

Bert's Italian Potato Salad

Owner: Bert Aluise (Don's Uncle)
Servings: 4
Prep Time: 10 minutes
Total Time: 15 minutes

. . . .

Ingredients:

4 medium potatoes, boiled whole until fork tender
Parsley
1/4 cup extra virgin olive oil
1/4 cup green onions
1/4 cup white onions
Salt

Directions

Cut potatoes into cubes. Dice the onions and toss with potatoes. Add the oil, the salt, and the parsley. Mix and serve.

Tip:

This dish can either be served cold or hot. If you want to serve this as a hot dish, simply serve immediately mixing all of the ingredients together. The potatoes should be warm enough to conduct heat throughout the entire dish. If you want to serve this cold, cover and refrigerate after you have mixed all of the ingredients.

BBQ Chili

Owner: Collin
Servings: 6
Prep Time: 30 minutes
Total Time: 1 hour

. . . .

Ingredients:

1 pound ground turkey
2 cans diced tomatoes, with garlic and onion
2 cans chili beans, in medium spiced sauce
1 can tomato sauce
1 packet chili seasoning (spice level depending on your preference)
1-2 teaspoons cumin
1-2 teaspoons chipotle chili powder
3 cloves garlic, minced
2 teaspoons cinnamon
4 tablespoons BBQ sauce
1 tablespoon olive oil
Salt and pepper to taste

Directions

Brown ground turkey with olive oil in skillet. (Turkey can get a bit sticky on the bottom of the skillet; so make sure to use olive oil, adding more if you need it.) When the turkey is mostly done, add salt, pepper and cinnamon.

In a large pot over medium-high heat, add all ingredients. Cook for at least 20-30 minutes, stirring occasionally. Reduce temperature for another 20 minutes. (Chili is best when it simmers slowly for a while and next day leftovers are normally better than the first batch.) Serve with your favorite toppings (such as sour cream, chives, oyster crackers, cilantro, shredded cheese).

Bert's Beef Stew

Owner: Bert Aluise (Don's Uncle)
Servings: 8
Prep Time: 20 minutes
Total Time: 1 hour 20 minutes

. . . .

Ingredients:

1 pound beef steaks, cut into chunks
1/2 pound Italian sausage
3-4 carrots, chopped
1 stalk celery, chopped
4 potatoes
2 cups beef broth
Salt and pepper

Directions

Brown the beef and sausage in sauté pan.
Combine all ingredients in large stockpot.
Add broth and water; simmer for 1 hour.

Story:

Having had the opportunity to grow up in a Greek family meant several things. First it meant always being surrounded by a host of fun-loving, gregarious, happy family members, all of whom could cook and loved to eat too. Our family gatherings didn't have just good food as the centerpiece, but GREAT food.

With that Greek heritage, also came the Lebanese, the Italian, and even the good ol' American cuisine served at family dinners. As a kid reaching on tip toes to the dining room table, I could have easily pulled down a Greek Grape Leaf, homemade Italian Meatball or even my favorite Celery Stick filled with cream cheese dressing. And I may get into trouble naming favorites, but here goes.

My Aunt Ann & Uncle Bert were the Italian cuisine connection to the family and they both were vying for the top Italian Chef Hat! Italian Meatballs, Lasagna, Chicken Cacciatore, and Pasta all made from scratch...simply amazing! And usually sometime during or after the meal, the family would spend some time discussing who, (Ann or Bert) had made the best dish? Both winners in my book!

Many of the recipes that you'll find within these pages are straight from Uncle Bert's & Aunt Ann's kitchen. You'll not only enjoy the dish, but share good conversation and family memories, which always went hand in hand with any of our family dinners.

- Don

Light Southwest Chicken Corn Chowder

Owner: Anna & Collin
Servings: 6
Prep Time: 1 hour
Total Time: 1 hour & 30 minutes

Ingredients:

4 chicken breasts
8 ounces smoked turkey sausage
2 14-ounce cans black beans
1 14-ounce can creamed corn
1 14-ounce can sweet corn kernels
2 garlic cloves, finely chopped
1 tablespoon cumin, or more to taste
3 tablespoons butter
3 tablespoons flour
3 cups skim milk
1/2 cup red onion, diced
1/4 cup white onion, diced
1 4-ounce can green chiles
3 bay leaves
3 teaspoons fresh thyme
1 teaspoon chipotle chili powder
Salt and pepper to taste

Directions:

Boil chicken in large pot until thoroughly cooked, about 30 minutes. Shred chicken and set aside. Melt butter into large pot. Sauté onions until tender, about 5 minutes. Add green chile and cook for 2 minutes. Add flour and stir constantly. Let mixture slightly thicken, about 2 minutes. Add milk and bring to a boil. Add remaining ingredients. Let cook for 20 minutes. Serve with thick cuts of sourdough bread.

Story:

One cold winter evening, we realized that we hadn't
thought ahead to what we were going to have for dinner
that night. But, we didn't really want to go to the store.
So, this chowder recipe actually was an awesome "Pantry
Scavenger Hunt Dinner." We rummaged through our canned
goods and threw them in a pot. The green chiles were a
later addition, along with the turkey sausage. But, as one of
our first kitchen experiments, we were pretty happy with it.
It's now one of our favorites!

- Anna & Collin

Breakfast

Breakfast Casserole

Owner: Sandi
Servings: 8-10
Prep Time: 45 minutes
Total Time: 1 hour 45 minutes (plus refrigeration time)

•••••••••••••••••••••••••••••••

Ingredients:

2 pounds breakfast sausage
8-10 pieces of white bread
12-14 eggs, beaten with a fork
2 teaspoons ground mustard
2 pounds shredded cheddar cheese
Salt and pepper to taste

Directions:

Cook breakfast sausage in pan, grinding the sausage in
the pan. Drain sausage and place in large mixing bowl.
Cut bread into small cubed pieces. Add to bowl. Mix all
remaining ingredients in bowl and pour into non-stick
sprayed 9 x 13 glass pan.

Let set in the refrigerator overnight or at least 6 hours.
After casserole is refrigerated, preheat oven to 350
degrees F. Put casserole into oven for 1 hour. Let set about
15-20 minutes before serving.

Tip:

Serve this with fruit salad and you have a wonderful BIG breakfast with very little work *(except for the night before)*. This has become our family's "go-to" breakfast when we're all together.

Blueberry Muffins

Owner: Aly
Servings: 8 large or 16 small muffins
Prep Time: 15 minutes
Total Time: 35-40 minutes

Ingredients:

1 1/2 cups all-purpose flour
3/4 cup white sugar
1/2 teaspoon salt
2 teaspoons baking powder
1/3 cup vegetable oil
1/2 teaspoon vanilla
1 teaspoon grated lemon peel
1/3 cup buttermilk
1 1/2 cup fresh blueberries
(may use frozen)

Topping:
1/2 cup brown sugar
1/3 cup all-purpose flour
1/4 cup butter, cubed
1 1/2 teaspoons ground cinnamon

Directions:

Preheat Oven to 400 degrees F and place liners in your muffin pan. (If you do not have liners you can use a cooking spray, but I would recommend using the cups and only a little spray on the top of the pan.)

For Muffins:
Combine the flour, sugar, salt and baking powder. In a separate bowl, combine the oil, egg, vanilla, lemon peel and buttermilk. Slowly add dry mixture to liquid until fully incorporated. Fold in the blueberries. (Do this step right before you pour the batter.)

For Topping:
Combine all ingredients and mix with a fork.

Spoon batter into muffin pans, about 2/3 of the way up, and sprinkle with topping.
Bake for 20 to 25 minutes for large muffins. Bake 15-20 minutes for small muffins.

Tip:

For a lower fat recipe, use milk (even skim) in place of the buttermilk and forgo the topping.

Pancakes

Owner: Sandi

. . . .

Directions:

There are so many wonderful recipes for pancakes I won't share one with you because we've used so many. And, good pancakes are only a box recipe away. But I still wanted to share a couple of stories surrounding pancakes....

When Anna was in nursery school (age 4), the teacher had a cooking day.
They were going to make pancakes. The teacher asked the students if they knew how to make pancakes. Some of the students said, "yes, you add some flour," and "you put in some eggs," or "add some oily stuff". Anna, disgusted, raised her hand and said, "no, no, no....you go to the freezer. You get it out of the freezer. You put it on a plate, and then you put it in the microwave. You got your pancakes." What do they say? Out of the mouths of babes!

The other pancake story surrounds "change" day. When you are divorced, you have those days when the kids "change" from your house and go to their other parent's house. We call these days "change" days. For years, I would make pancakes on "change" day. This kind of became a tradition. It was a rather flimsy "constant" in the kids ever changing world. Even to this day, when the family is over and I make pancakes, someone will say, "oh, is it change day?" Anna's husband will even make pancakes for Anna on the days she has to leave to travel. I love that our little tradition has been reframed and it is a source of comfort for the kids. And we do love our pancakes!

Bacon Maple Doughnuts

Owner: Aly
Servings: 1 dozen rings and centers
Prep Time: 20 minutes
Total Time: 50 minutes

Ingredients:

The doughnut :

3 cups all purpose flour (you may need a little
extra, but no more than a couple of
tablespoons)
1 package instant yeast
5 tablespoons sugar
1/2 teaspoon salt
2/3 cups whole milk, room temperature
2 large eggs, beaten lightly
6 tablespoons butter; soft but cool
3 cups oil for frying

Glaze:

1 1/4 cups powdered sugar
1 teaspoon vanilla
1/3 cup pure maple syrup
(make sure to get the good stuff!)

Bacon:

6 pieces of bacon, fully cooked and crumbled
into small pieces

Directions:

Doughnuts:
You will need a mixer with a dough hook attachment and a doughnut cutter.

In a bowl, combine the flour, yeast, sugar and salt. Set aside.

In the mixer bowl, place the milk and eggs. Add in the flour mixture and set on low speed. Mix until a dough ball forms. Add in the butter, 1 tablespoon at a time. Wait until each piece is incorporated, about 15 seconds. This is where you may need to use some extra flour. Add in the flour a tablespoon at a time, if necessary, until the dough becomes a soft ball.

Lightly oil a medium sized bowl, place the dough inside, and cover with plastic. Let the dough rise until it doubles in size. This will take about 2 hours.

Once the dough has risen, place it on a floured surface and roll it out with a rolling pin into 1/2 inch thickness.

Cut the dough with the doughnut cutter of your choice. (2 1/2 to 3 inches works best. They leave a decent sized center so you have doughnut holes!) Lightly flour a baking sheet and place the rings and centers on the sheet to rise for about 30 minutes. Cover them loosely with plastic.

Add the oil to a flat bottom saucepan and bring it to 375 degrees F. Use a candy thermometer to ensure that your oil stays at the correct temperature. You will be shallow frying the doughnuts, so they will never be fully covered in the oil. Place the doughnuts in 5 at a time. Fry until golden; each side will take about 30 seconds for the centers, and 50 seconds for the rings. When the doughnuts are done, drain them on a paper towel.

Make sure that the oil gets back up to the correct temperature between batches. Let the doughnuts cool for at least 10 minutes.

Maple Glaze:
Whisk together all ingredients until combined.

Assembly:
Dip the doughnuts in the glaze. Let them set for about 15 seconds, and then crumble the bacon on top. Enjoy!

Quiche with Turkey Bacon & Zucchini

Owner: Anna
Servings: 6 slices
Prep Time: 15 minutes
Total Time: 30 minutes

Ingredients:

1 pie crust
6 slices turkey bacon, cut into small pieces
1 medium zucchini
1/2 cup red onion, diced
5 egg whites
3 eggs
1/4 cup whipping cream
1/2 cup no fat sour cream
3/4 cup skim milk
2/3 cup gruyere cheese, grated
Salt and pepper

Directions:

Set oven to 375 degrees F. Roll out piecrust into prepared spring form cake or pie pan. (Make sure it is not a shallow pan, as mixture will expand in the oven.) Poke holes in the bottom and sides of piecrust with fork. Bake for 15 minutes or until slightly golden brown. While piecrust is baking, sauté bacon, zucchini and onion. Place sauté in bowl and set aside. In an electric mixer, mix in one egg at a time, combining the whipping cream, skim milk and sour cream slowly. Mix until smooth. Add remaining ingredients to bowl, including sauté, and mix well. Take piecrust out of the oven and pour mixture into the crust. Bake 45-55 minutes or until quiche is set.   Cool for 15 minutes, cut and serve.

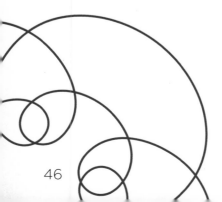

Bacon, Egg & Cheese Burger

Owner: Donnie
Servings: 6 burgers
Prep Time: 16 minutes
Total Time: 27 minutes

Ingredients:

2 pounds ground beef (makes 6 1/3-pound patties)
6 eggs
6 strips pepper bacon
Salt and pepper
6 burger buns of your choice

Directions:

Divide the beef into 6 even pieces and flatten to patties. Salt and pepper both sides of each patty. You can grill these or sauté them. They will cook about 6 minutes for each side. Cook to your preference.

Once your burgers are done embellish them with the eggs and bacon. Cook these the way you normally would in a skillet.

Story:

I love breakfast. I just have a hard time waking up in time to enjoy it. I've seen this burger at a couple restaurants and wanted to try to make it on my own. I like to use pepper bacon to add a little more flavor to the sandwich. You can make the egg however you like, but I prefer over-medium so there's still some yolk. Trust me, this burger is the best when the yolk runs all over the burger.

– Donnie

Monkey Bread

Owner: Collin
Servings: 8
Prep Time: 20 minutes
Total Time: 1 hour

Ingredients:

4 cans refrigerated biscuits
1 3/4 cup sugar
3 tsp cinnamon
3/4 cup butter

Directions:

Heat oven to 350 degrees F. Prepare Bundt or tube pan with non-stick coating. In a small bowl, combine half of the cinnamon and 3/4 cup sugar. Cut each biscuit into quarters and coat with cinnamon and sugar mixture. (It's best to make sure each quarter gets a good coating. Don't coat the whole mix at the same time.) Drop each biscuit piece into pan. Set aside. In a small saucepan, combine remaining ingredients and bring to a boil over medium-high heat on stove. Pour over biscuits in pan. Bake for 40-45 minutes, or until golden brown. Turn pan over on plate and serve.

Story:

You may have heard of Monkey Bread before. Maybe you've even had the good fortune of enjoying this delicacy. The origin of Monkey Bread is somewhat unclear, but one thing is certain: it's good. There are many variations to this delicious dish, none quite as good as this recipe, though. Many have scoffed at Monkey Bread, calling it a glorified glob of donut holes, or just a simple recipe of biscuits, sugar, and butter. While the recipe may be simple, the experience of enjoying Monkey Bread is far from it.

Monkey Bread wasn't necessarily a 'special occasion' dish in the Trent household when I was a child, but it wasn't exactly an everyday fixture, either. You see, Monkey Bread is somewhat of a labor of love. And while my mom loved us very much, she juggled many responsibilities; Monkey Bread not always being at the top of that list. Monkey Bread requires more than just taking biscuits out of the can and covering them with sugar and cinnamon. It requires precise separation of each biscuit into quarters, then giving each piece individual attention by blanketing it with a fine coating of cinnamon and sugar, and finally covering it with the right amount of glaze.

Though not strictly a weekend treat, more often than not Monkey Bread seemed to grace our house on Saturday mornings. With church on Sundays, and the weekday mornings being interrupted by school and work, Saturday mornings were an ideal time for a good breakfast. Once the hours of a Friday evening called my siblings and I to bed, my mom would do much of the preparation so as to not make us wait too long for breakfast once we woke up the next day. Waking-up to the smell of baking Monkey Bread was second only to Christmas morning. The sweet smell of cinnamon, sugar, butter, and my mom's loving touch filled our house and soon the perfectly-baked dough filled our bellies. It often started out with my brother and I wrestling for first grabs and our older sister scoffing at us with disgust, but the result was a breakfast enjoyed by all and a dish that will forever be enjoyed by the Trent family.

Though my siblings and I are now married and beginning families of our own, our mom's Monkey Bread is still a welcomed treat over holidays or other occasions when we find ourselves under our parent's roof. Even on the morning of my wedding, my mom found a way to make Monkey Bread for me. Though the entire day was perfect, beginning the morning with this cherished family tradition seemed to be fitting as I embarked on this new journey in life.

Monkey Bread is a dish with few ingredients. For me, though, the memories and emotions it conjures-up are far from few. I hope you're able to enjoy this dish. Feel free to put your own spin on it; add some nuts, dried fruit, whatever you'd like! As with many recipes, the final product is not always about the dish itself, rather the memories created because of it.

– Collin

Pasta

Ugly Green Ogre Pesto Pasta

Owner: Aly
Servings: 8
Prep Time: 10-15
Total Time: 30 minutes

. . . .

Story:

This is a simple recipe that has a sweet story along with it. The first time I made this recipe I was experimenting with making Pesto. I loved pesto and knew that it would be something simple and worthwhile to master. I scoured the Internet for tips, and pairings, and finally settled on creating my own. I would make pasta, with shrimp. Easy peasy. So I made the dish, and as I was serving it, my youngest half-sister, Sydney, exclaimed that the pasta looked like a certain ugly green ogre she so loved from her movies...You know who I'm talking about. So here you have "Ugly Green Ogre Pasta." I began my pesto-perfecting journey with this recipe, and am still using it seven years later today.

- C Aly

Ingredients:

2 1/2 cups (firmly packed) Fresh Basil Leaves
4 cloves Garlic
2 tablespoons pine nuts
1/2 cup to 1 cup Parmesan/Romano Cheese
Olive Oil
Salt to taste

1 lb. linguini (or whatever pasta you choose)
1 lb. Uncooked Shrimp (Fresh or frozen. Sometimes frozen is better than what "fresh" you might have available at your local grocery store.)

Directions:

Start by toasting your pine nuts in a skillet with a little olive oil. This brings out a lovely nutty flavor that you don't get with right out of the jar pine nuts. Add in your basil, garlic, and pine nuts to a food processor. Turn on and slowly add in olive oil until you get a nice creamy texture. Add in cheese and pulse until combined.

If you used frozen shrimp, thaw your shrimp by placing in a colander and running cold water over the shrimp. Make sure that all of your shrimp are cleaned, shelled, and de-veined. If you bought from a fishmonger you can ask them to do this for you. Place shrimp in a skillet with enough oil to coat bottom of pan. Let cook until tails curl and shrimp are slightly pink. Do not over cook! Shrimp so easily get rubbery that you have to be careful. Your shrimp should be the last thing you cook. You can make your pasta throughout and by the time you are finished with prep and preparing, it should be done.

Cook pasta until al dente. Drain pasta, but reserve a cup of the pasta water. Add in a quarter cup of the pasta water to the pesto and then toss with pasta. Add the shrimp and voila! You have an easy, and delicious pesto masterpiece!

Tip:

The thing about pesto is that you really cannot go wrong with the amount of ingredients.
If you like more garlic, then add more garlic. If you like less cheese, or you like a smoother pesto change the amounts. Play around with it.

Rabbit Pasta

Owner: Andrew (Aly's boyfriend)
Servings: 4
Prep Time: 15
Total Time: 25 minutes

. . . .

Ingredients:

1 half box (or 6 ounces) penne pasta
1/4 cup olive oil
6 cloves garlic
1 tablespoon red pepper flakes
1 12-ounce can crushed tomatoes
Salt and pepper

Directions:

Cook the pasta per the package instructions.
While the pasta water is heating up, sauté
the garlic and the red pepper flakes in the
olive oil on medium high heat until the garlic
is golden. Immediately add the tomatoes and
stir to combine. Turn the heat down to
medium low, stirring occasionally. Salt and
pepper to taste.

Story:

My family has always loved Italian food, and
that is especially true of pasta. We have
always had many different pasta recipes, and
Rabbit Pasta is one of my favorites. Although
people are always taken off guard by the
name, the dish does not include any rabbit-
-or any other meat for that matter. Instead,
it is based on an older recipe called 'pasta el
rabitto,' and it is quite spicy. Enjoy!

Bacon Sun Dried Tomato Alfredo

Owner: Aly
Servings: 4-6 (2 cups total)
Prep Time: 10 minutes
Total Time: 30 minutes

Ingredients:

1 cup heavy cream
1 1/2 cup parmesan/Romano cheese
1/2 stick butter
2 cloves garlic, minced
1/2 cup diced sun dried tomatoes (not in oil)
8 slices bacon (cut into 1/2 inch pieces)

Directions

Sauté bacon until slightly crispy. Remove from pan and set aside. Drain the fat from the pan and return to stove.

Sauté sun dried tomatoes until color has darkened and they are soft. Remove from pan and set aside. Add cream and butter to sauté pan and bring to a simmer. Quickly whisk in garlic and cheese. Return bacon and sun dried tomatoes to pan. Serve over pasta and some grilled chicken or use as a base for an awesome pizza!

Bert's Lemon Chicken Alfredo

Owner: Bert Aluise (Don's Uncle)
Servings: 8-10
Prep Time: 30 minutes
Total Time: 1 hour 30 minutes

Ingredients:

1 large frying chicken
Large lemon
1 box fettuccini pasta
Salt and pepper

For Alfredo Sauce:
1 cup chicken broth
1/2 cup sautéed onions
2 cloves garlic, minced
1 tablespoon parsley
1 cup grated parmesan or Romano cheese
1 cup half and half
1 teaspoon corn starch
1 teaspoon cold water

For Herb Butter:
1 cup butter, softened (but still cold)
1 tablespoon parsley
1 tablespoon chopped chives
1 tablespoon basil
2 teaspoons thyme
1 teaspoon lemon pepper
2 cloves garlic, minced

Directions:

Preheat oven to 350 degrees F.

Mix all ingredients for herb butter in small bowl. Coat the chicken in the butter. Poke holes throughout the lemon and place inside chicken. Bake for 1 hour.

Strain sauce from chicken and place in a saucepan over medium heat. Add the chicken broth, onions, garlic and parsley. Stir until combined.

Cook pasta according to package instructions.

In a separate bowl, combine the cornstarch and the cold water. Mix well and then add to the broth mixture. Wisk to combine. Wisk in cheese and half and half to the broth mixture and heat.

Shred or cut up the chicken. Add to sauce, and serve with cooked fettuccini pasta.

Light Spaghetti

Owner: Sandi

Servings: 6-8

Prep Time: 20-25 minutes

Total Time: 30-45 minutes

Ingredients:

2 tablespoons olive oil
2 lb lean ground turkey or chicken
2 teaspoons fennel seed
2 cloves garlic, finely chopped
1/2 large white onion, diced
1 (24 ounce approx) large jar of your favorite spaghetti sauce. You can use more or less depending on the amount of people you are serving and how thick you want the sauce.
1 lb whole wheat spaghetti

Directions:

Over medium heat, add oil and brown turkey or chicken in large saucepan. After meat has cooked about 5 minutes, add the fennel seed, garlic and white onion. Drain and add spaghetti sauce. Cover and let simmer over medium-low heat.

While sauce is simmering, cook spaghetti per package instructions. Top pasta with meat sauce. Serve immediately and Bon Appetit!

Tip:

The fennel seed is the secret ingredient in the turkey. Cooking with ground turkey or chicken is a healthy adjustment I've made in my diet. But, I always missed the flavor of Italian sausage. That flavor is in the fennel. With that, and the other spices, you'll never know you're eating something other than Italian sausage. Use these spices when you want to add a little "Italiano" flavor.

Easy Chicken Lasagna

Owner: Aly
Servings: 8
Prep Time: 20 minutes
Total Time: 45 minutes

Ingredients:

1 pound chicken breast
2 boxes of lasagna noodles
1 26-ounce jar of your favorite pasta sauce (or
homemade if you have a great recipe)
3 cloves, garlic, minced
2 1/2 cups parmesan and/or Romano cheese, grated
2 cups ricotta cheese
1 tablespoon oregano
Salt and pepper
2 tablespoons olive oil

Directions:

Preheat oven to 350 degree F.

Begin by preparing your pasta sheets by the package. (Most packages say to cook
your pasta halfway so that when you put it in the oven it cooks the rest of the way).

Cut the chicken into small pieces. Sauté with the olive oil, oregano, garlic, salt and pepper until you have
a nice golden sear on all sides.
In a separate bowl, combine the 2 cups ricotta and 2 cups grated cheeses. Set aside.
Layer ingredients into a 12x9 baking dish. Place lasagna sheets, enough to cover the bottom of the pan,
on the bottom. Top with half of the chicken, pasta sauce and cheese mixture. Repeat layer, starting
again with the lasagna noodles, and then place an additional layer of lasagna. Add remaining sauce and
1/2 cup grated cheese on top.

Bake in oven for 20 minutes. Let lasagna rest for about 5-10 minutes before serving.

Grill

Tip:

I can't say it enough; be creative! You can put anything you want on the inside of these burgers. Whether it is one of the combos I mentioned, or just one of your favorites. Make a bunch of burgers, forget which ones they are, and have a fun time being surprised with each bite.

Donnie's Stuffed Burgers

Owner: Donnie

Prep Time: 10 minutes

Servings: 6 burgers

Total Time: 25 minutes

Ingredients:

2 pounds ground beef (preferably 80/20 beef)
6 thin cheese slices of your choice (such as American, Colby-jack, pepper-jack)
1 teaspoon garlic powder
1/2 teaspoon pepper
1/2 teaspoon salt
1 tablespoon Worcestershire sauce
6 buns of your choice

Directions:

Add garlic, pepper, salt and Worcestershire sauce to the ground beef in a large mixing bowl. Mix well with your hands. Divide the ground beef into 6 pieces. Then divided each of those in half and flatten to patties. (You must be careful not to over work the meat or it will get tough.) Cut each cheese slice into 4 pieces and stack in the middle of 6 of the patties. Take the remaining patties and place one on top of each of the ones with cheese. Pinch together the edges to create a good seal. Heat grill to medium-high heat. Grill each side for about 6 minutes.

Your burgers may develop a steam bubble. If this happens, after you have flipped it once poke a hole in the top to let some of the steam out.

Grilled Chipotle Lime Chicken

Owner: Aly
Servings: 4-6
Prep Time: 25 minutes
Total Time: 35 minutes

Ingredients:

6 pieces of chicken (breast, leg or thigh)
1 tablespoon chipotle powder
1/4 cup lime juice
1 teaspoon lime zest
1 clove garlic, minced
1/2 cup plain yogurt
2 tablespoons honey
Salt and pepper, to taste

Directions:

Mix together all of the ingredients, except the chicken and the honey. Set aside 1/4 cup of mixture. Spread remaining marinade over chicken and allow to sit in refrigerator for 20 minutes.

Grill chicken skin side down for 8 to 10 minutes until chicken is cooked. Add the honey to the 1/4 cup of sauce and spread over chicken, as chicken is continuing to cook on the grill. Cook for 1 or 2 more minutes then remove from grill. Serve and enjoy.

Tip:

Don is the master griller. Really, he is fabulous. You can give him anything and it's always better on the grill. There are lots of "cook on the grill" recipes so we will just give you some tips that work great for Don.

First tip for grilling, keep a spray water bottle handy. From time to time throughout the grilling process, spray water directly on to whatever you are grilling. This keeps any meat you are cooking from drying out. The other thing we have discovered is that if you are grilling chicken, cook it for just about 15 min in the oven at 350 degrees F. Then finish it on the grill. Chicken dries out so easily and by cooking it a bit in the oven, it keeps it juicy and then tossing it on the grill to finish it makes it perfection!

- Sandi

Sam's Barbeque Ribs

Owner: Sam
Servings: 2-3
Prep Time: 10 minutes
Total Time: 1 hour 10 minutes

Ingredients:

1 1/2 lbs spare ribs
1 bottle of your favorite barbeque sauce
2-4 teaspoons hot sauce
(more if you like it spicy)
1/2 teaspoon–1 teaspoon liquid smoke
2 tablespoons honey
2 tablespoons brown sugar

Directions:

Place spare ribs on foil lined baking sheet. Mix remaining ingredients in medium bowl. Brush mixture evenly on all ribs, leaving about 1/4 of mixture. Place ribs on heated grill. Brush spare ribs throughout cooking process. Cook until tender. Place ribs back on baking sheet and place in warm oven to keep ribs tender.

Story:

Ever since Sam was a little guy, he has loved working in the kitchen and getting his hands dirty. He has had great teachers too, as he has learned to make everything from chocolate chip cookies to burgers on the grill. Sam especially loves barbeque ribs. One day, he and his buddy Chandler decided that as a part of their fundraiser for their baseball team they would make slabs of ribs and sell them on the side of the road. No lemonade stand for these guys. So we ran to a local wholesale store, bought a few slabs of ribs, and Sammo whipped together a fabulous homemade barbeque sauce. (He totally made it up the first time!) Dad set up a grill on the side of the road, and WOW, they sold some ribs. People screeched to a halt to buy slabs of ribs for dinner. It was awesome, and they made some money for their baseball team. And that, ladies and gentlemen, is how it gets done.

Main Dish

Reduced Fat Enchiladas

Owner: Anna
Servings: 6
Prep Time: 30 minutes
Total Time: 1 hour

Ingredients:

6 large tortillas
4 chicken breasts, cut into small strips
1/2 cup red onion, diced
1/4 cup cilantro leaves, chopped
1/2 cup non-fat sour cream
1 12-ounce can cream of chicken soup, reduced fat
1 cup shredded Mexican blend cheese
1 12-ounce can black beans
1 12-ounce can sweet corn kernels
1 4-ounce can green chiles
1 8-ounce can diced tomatoes, with Mexican seasoning
1 12-ounce can green chile enchilada sauce
2 packets taco seasonings
2 tablespoon olive oil
Salt and pepper to taste

Directions:

Heat oven to 400 degrees F. Cut chicken into small strips and sauté, with olive oil, in non-stick pan until thoroughly cooked. Season with salt and pepper, if desired. Mix all ingredients, except for tortillas, 1/2 cup cheese and enchilada sauce, into large bowl. Spray 9 x 13 inch glass pan with cooking spray. Place tortilla in pan, fill with 1/6 mixture, roll up, folds sides in and secure in pan. Repeat with the remaining tortillas. Bake for 20 minutes. Take out pan and pour enchilada sauce and remaining cheese on top of tortillas. Bake for an additional 15 minutes. Take out of oven and serve.

Story:

This recipe is a spin on my favorite enchiladas that are made by our friend, Kim Williams. Our families get together every year and make Christmas cookies. Now these are some serious cookies. We're talking pretzel support systems for tri-level cookies and a serious judging panel at the end of the evening. But, the meal that gets us going is her amazing enchiladas. She serves it with guacamole and the best Mexican corn cake bake thing... It's amazing! So enjoy these enchiladas and make some awesome Christmas cookies.

- Anna

Salmon Patties

Owner: Sandi
Servings: 5-7
Prep Time: 20 minutes
Total Time: 40 minutes

Ingredients:

4 6-ounce cans of Salmon
(without skin and bones)
2 eggs beaten
16 saltine crackers crushed
3 to 4 tablespoons of oil in the frying pan
Salt & pepper to taste

Directions:

In medium size bowl, mix salmon, beaten eggs, crushed crackers and seasoning to taste. Mix well. Mixture will be wet (and that's a good thing). Form into 2-inch size "patties". Place in heated pan that has heated oil. Add salmon patties and cook about 10 minutes, turn, cook another 10 minutes. Serve.

Story:

When I first began my career, I also started a kids club called the Friendship Company. There were thousands of kids who became part of the Friendship Company. One day I got a letter from a mom whose daughter was in the Friendship Company. She just had to tell me a story. The night before this mom had made Salmon Patties for her family for dinner. When she called the family to dinner and announced what they were having, the little girl said in a bewildered voice, "Mommy, we can't eat Sandi Patty's for dinner. She's with the Friendship Company". How adorable. Now our Salmon Patties, which my mom has made for years, are often referred to as Sandi Patty's.

- Sandi

These salmon patties go great with a big dollop of ketchup and fried potatoes. YUM!

Lasagna Loaf

Owner: Sandi
Servings: 4-6
Prep Time: 20 minutes
Total Time: 40 minutes

. . . .

Ingredients:

1/2 pound ground beef
1/2 pound sausage
6 ounces tomato paste
1 teaspoon garlic powder
1/2 cup chopped onion
1/2 teaspoon basil flakes
1/2 teaspoon parsley
1/2 teaspoon oregano
1 cup cottage cheese
1 egg
1/4 cup Parmesan cheese
3 large slices mozzarella
2 cans crescent rolls

Directions:

Brown ground beef and sausage. Salt and pepper to taste. Add onion and spices. Drain and add tomato paste. Preheat oven to 350 degrees F. In another bowl, combine cottage cheese, egg and parmesan. Mix well. Roll out first can of crescent rolls onto foil-lined, greased cookie sheet. Spread half of meat mixture, all of sauce, and the other half of meat mixture on top, layering it on top. Top with mozzarella and the second can of crescent rolls. Pinch together the edges of the rolls and brush the top with milk. Sprinkle with sesame seeds to add some texture. Bake 20 minutes or until crescent roll is fully cooked and golden brown.

Baked Pork Chops

Owner: Betty Fair
(longtime friend and nanny of the kids)
Servings: 8-10
Prep Time: 20 minutes
Total Time: 50 minutes

. . . .

Ingredients:

8 small pork chops
2 eggs, beaten
Saltine crackers, crushed to crumbs
Flour, enough to cover each piece pork
6 tablespoons butter or margarine

Directions

Preheat oven to 350 degrees F. Sprinkle salt and pepper well. Roll each piece in the flour then dip in the eggs. Coat the pork with cracker crumbs and place in shallow baking dish. After all of the pieces are prepped, pour the melted butter over the top. Bake until pork is cooked through for approximately 30 minutes.

"Fried" Pork Chops

Owner: Sandi
Servings: 6
Prep Time: 30 minutes
Total Time: 1 hour 30 minutes

. . . .

Ingredients:

6 butterfly pork chops
2 cans cream of mushroom soup
1/2 cup milk
1 cup flour
2 teaspoon garlic salt
2 teaspoon onion salt
Salt pepper to taste
1/2 cup of vegetable oil

Directions

Preheat oven at 350 degrees F. Place vegetable oil in pan over medium-high heat to warm oil. Make a flour mixture with about 1/2 flour, garlic salt, pepper. Coat pork chops in flour mixture and place in hot oil. Cook on both sides for about 3 min each. Place seared pork chops in baking dish. Cover with cream of mushroom soup. Cook in oven for about 1 hour.

Chicken & Cashew Casserole

Owner: Betty Fair
(longtime friend and nanny of the kids)
Servings: 4
Prep Time: 10 minutes
Total Time: 1 hour 10 minutes

. . . .

Ingredients:

1 can chicken, cooked, boned and diced
1 can cream of mushroom soup
3/4 cup chicken broth
2 tablespoons onion, chopped
1 cup chopped celery
1/2 can chow mein noodles
1/2 cup frozen mixed vegetables
1/2 cup cashew nuts
2 teaspoons poultry seasoning
1 teaspoon paprika
Salt and pepper

Directions

Preheat oven to 325 degrees F. Cook celery and onion in microwave for 2 minutes. In large bowl, combine all ingredients, including cooked celery and onion, and mix until incorporated.

Place in greased baking dish and bake for 1 hour.

Fish Tacos

Owner: Aly
Servings: 4
Prep Time: 30 minutes
Total Time: 90 minutes

Directions :

1 pound white fish, cut into chunks (The chunks do not have to be any particular size. You can use cod, halibut, mahi-mahi, whatever you like.)

Breaded Fish:
1 cup all-purpose flour
2 tablespoons cornstarch
1 teaspoon baking powder
1 egg
1 cup stock (either mushroom, chicken or beef)
1/2 teaspoon salt
1/4 teaspoon pepper
Oil, for frying

In a bowl, combine flour, cornstarch, baking powder, salt and pepper. Blend egg and stock in a separate bowl and then quickly stir into the flour mixture. Heat oil to 375 degrees F in heavy bottomed pan, deep fryer or Dutch oven. Lightly flour the fish and then dip in batter. Fry until golden brown. Place on paper towel to drain.

Sautéed Fish:
1/4 cup olive oil
1 1/2 teaspoon chipotle powder
1/2 teaspoon cumin
1/4 cup cilantro, chopped
Salt and pepper

Combine ingredients, mix well, and place aside. Place fish in shallow baking dish and pour marinade on top. Allow mixture to sit for 15 minutes. Sauté fish in a non-stick skillet on medium heat. Sear each side for approximately 3-4 minutes.

Chipotle Aioli:
1/2 cup mayonnaise
1 1/2 tablespoon chives, finely chopped
2 garlic cloves, minced
1 teaspoon lime juice
1 teaspoon chipotle powder
Salt and pepper

Add ingredients into a bowl, and stir. Refrigerate until ready to serve.

Pico de Gallo:
1 large tomato or 2 small tomatoes, cut into small cubes
2 tablespoons lime juice
1/2 cup cilantro, chopped
1/2 cup avocado, cut into small cubes
1/4 cup red onion, finely chopped
3 cloves garlic, minced
1/2 teaspoon salt

Chop, chop, chop! Combine the tomato, cilantro, red onion, garlic, lime juice and salt. Mix together. Add in the avocado and give it another quick stir. Let sit in refrigerator for at least an hour. The longer it sets, the better the flavor will be.

Tip:

Tacos can be served with many different toppings, but these are my favorites. You can heat your tortillas however you like. Choose your fish, add a little lettuce or chopped cabbage, add the Pico and then the Aioli. The sauce is killer. If you are a sauce lover, you should double the recipe.

Tip:
The remaining meat makes great barbeque beef sandwiches the next day. Just add a little BBQ sauce and serve on Kaiser rolls.

Sandi's Easy Pot Roast

Owner: Sandi
Servings: 6-8
Prep Time: 5 minutes
Total Time: 6-8 hours

Ingredients:

8-10 lb lean pot roast (frozen)
1 package dry onion soup mix
2/3 cup water
4 cans baby carrots (or 4 cups carrots chopped)
4 cans whole potatoes (or 4 cups potatoes chopped)
Salt and pepper to taste

Story:

I always tried to fix nice dinners but I never really had the time. This Pot Roast I made one day out of desperation. It's so easy and really good. Do this first thing in the morning before school or work and it cooks all day. We often serve green beans with the roast.

– Sandi

Directions:

Preheat oven to 350 degrees F. Place frozen roast in roasting pan. Mix one package of onion soup mix and water and pour over roast. Cover with foil and place in oven. Let roast cook for about 4 hours until the meat begins to darken. Remove roast and add cans of vegetables along with the water. (The vegetables are already cooked so they don't need very much time.) Place roast back in oven and cook for 2-4 more hours. (Continuously check on roast until desired temperature.) Make sure the center of the roast is done and serve.

BBQ Shrimp

Owner: Andrew (Aly's boyfriend)
Servings: 4
Prep Time: 5 minutes
Total Time: 5 minutes

Ingredients:

1 pound shrimp (uncooked, without shell)
6 cloves garlic, chopped
1 shallot, chopped
1 tablespoon chili powder
1 tablespoon brown sugar
1 teaspoon cumin
1 teaspoon salt
1/2 teaspoon pepper
3 tablespoons olive oil

Tip:

The cast iron skillet is the key to getting the flavor of recipe. Technically speaking, it conducts heat evenly. Deliciously speaking, it just spreads the flavor around much better. Make sure to use the recommended cleaning procedure that came with your skillet, because of the way in which the pan is treated.

This recipe goes great with the cheesy grits listed on page 102. Your very own "shrimp and grits."

Directions:

Combine all but the shrimp and the garlic in a bowl to make the rub for the shrimp.
Then stir in the shrimp to make sure each one gets a coat. On high heat, add the oil to a cast iron skillet. Sauté the garlic until golden, then add the shallot and shrimp. Cook until shrimp are bright in color, about 4-5 minutes.

Pork Roast

Owner: Jenn
Servings: 8-12
Prep Time: 30 minutes
Total Time: 2 hours

Ingredients:

1 medium-sized pork loin, or tail
1/4 cup dried cranberries
1/4 cup goat cheese
1/2 cup spinach leaves
4 slices mozzarella cheese
2 tablespoons rosemary
2 tablespoons thyme
Salt and pepper
Olive oil
Twine, to secure pork

Directions

Preheat oven to 350 degrees F. Butterfly pork. Place all ingredients in the pork, scattering the ingredients evenly. Roll up the pork to close the gap with the ingredients. Wrap twine around the entire pork loin and secure by tying the twine. Coat the loin in olive oil and sprinkle with Kosher salt and pepper. Place loin in a large pan. (Use a pan that is deep enough to handle natural juices that will seep out of the pork.) Bake for 1 hour 30 minutes or until internal temperature is at least 160 degrees F. Let the pork rest for about 10 minutes. Cut off the twine. Cut pork into slices and serve.

Story:

Spaghetti squash is a great alternative to pasta. It's a vegetable, and vegetables are always good for you, and it happens to take on any flavor that you're cooking with. Use it in place of pasta or rice if you're looking for a low carb option. And, this recipe works well with pretty much any kind of meat and vegetable so have fun with the recipe!

- Anna & Collin

Spaghetti Squash Italian

Owner: Anna & Collin
Servings: 4-6
Prep Time: 1 hour
Total Time: 1 hour 30 minutes

Ingredients:

1 spaghetti squash
4 chicken breasts
Sliced mushrooms
1 medium zucchini
1/2 cup parmesan cheese
3 cloves garlic, minced
3 tablespoons olive oil
1/2 cup white cooking wine
1/4 cup lemon juice
1/2 cup chicken stock
2 tablespoons basil, plus more to taste
2 tablespoons oregano, plus more to taste
Salt and pepper
2 cups of fresh spinach

Directions:

Preheat oven to 350 degrees F. Cut squash in half (cutting through the long side of the squash). Remove seeds. Place both halves cut side down on baking sheet. Bake for 45 minutes. Let squash cool for about 15 minutes. Using a fork, scrap out the squash from the skin and place in bowl. (The squash will actually look like spaghetti noodles when it's scraped out.) Season with salt and pepper. Set aside.

Cut chicken breasts into long strips. Place in large skillet. Add olive oil and cook chicken for about 5 minutes on medium-high heat. Add garlic, basil, oregano, salt and pepper and cook for another 5 minutes. Add zucchini and mushrooms. Season as desired with same ingredients. Add cooking wine and lemon juice and cook for 10 additional minutes, or until chicken is fully cooked. (Feel free to add more liquid depending on how much "sauce" you want.)

Place spaghetti squash in skillet and mix all ingredients together, adding seasonings to your taste. Serve in large bowls.

Baked Chicken Fingers

Owner: Mollie
Servings: 8
Prep Time: 10
Total Time: 30 minutes

Ingredients:

8 chicken breasts
2 cups breadcrumbs (Italian style works)
1/2 cup parmesan cheese
2 teaspoons garlic powder
1/2 teaspoon salt
1/4 teaspoon black pepper
3 eggs beaten

Directions:

Preheat oven to 400 degrees F. Slice each chicken breast into 4 strips. In a shallow dish, combine the breadcrumbs, cheese, garlic powder, salt and pepper. Dredge each chicken piece in the eggs, making sure that the extra drips off. (If you don't do this, the breading will slip off.) Place chicken finger on a foil lined baking sheet. Bake for 10 minutes and turn over. Continue baking another 10 minutes, or until chicken is cooked through.

Story:

If I had to choose one food to eat for the rest of my life, it would be chicken fingers. Correction-it would be chicken fingers with a huge side helping of Ranch dressing. In my opinion, everything is better with Ranch. Since I was a little girl I absolutely loved these fried goodies. But, they're not always the healthiest things to eat. My solution is to bake the chicken fingers instead of fry them. And it tastes great! I still like this with Ranch dressing, but there are great low-fat and fat-free Ranch options out there. Enjoy!

- Mollie

Mom's Magnificent Meatloaf

Owner: Sandi
Servings: 5-7
Prep Time: 15 minutes

....

Ingredients:

2-3 pounds lean ground beef or ground chuck
1 small box of Grape Nut Flakes
1 small onion chopped
2 eggs, beaten
Salt, pepper and garlic powder to season
1 cup lite pancake syrup
2 tablespoons mustard
1/2 cup ketchup

Directions

Mix together the ground beef, onion, eggs and Grape Nut flakes (just enough flakes to hold the loaf together) and seasonings. (The best way to mix these ingredients is to do it by hand. A little messy but it makes a difference.) In a separate bowl, mix syrup, ketchup and mustard and pour 1/2 into meat mixture.

Spray an iron skillet with cooking spray. Put meat into skillet (mound in the middle). Poke holes with the handle of a wooden spoon into meat loaf. Pour remaining syrup mixture over meat loaf. Bake at 350 degrees F for about 1-2 hours until top is brown and crisp. (Length of time may vary according to the amount of meat used.)

Story:

You can get a lot of food when you are traveling and on the road but the one thing I have found that I really can't get anywhere is a good meatloaf. I LOVE meatloaf. It is probably my ultimate comfort food. So when I come home from being on the road for a while, that is the first thing I make. Meatloaf. To accompany the rest of the meal, I like baked potatoes with all the fixin's—sour cream, butter, grated cheese, bacon bits. And although most of my family doesn't like it, I make peas. I love little baby peas. Again, not something you can get just anywhere. And then of course I put ketchup on the meatloaf. The best part is the next day. I love me some meatloaf sandwich. Ultimate goodness, ultimate comfort.

- Sandi

Make Your Own Pizza

Owner: Family
Servings: 1 personal pizza
Prep Time: 10 minutes
Total Time: 20 minutes

Ingredients:

Store bought, pre-cooked personal pizza crust
Canned sauce (such as marinara sauce, alfredo
sauce, olive oil)
Grated cheese (such as really fresh mozzarella,
goat cheese, manchego)
Variety of vegetables (such as tomatoes, onions,
peppers, mushrooms)
Variety of meats (such as pepperoni, sausage,
chicken, ham, bacon)
Additional toppings (such as pineapple,
artichokes, crushed red pepper flakes,
sun-dried tomatoes)

Story:

Making dinner together is a very fun family activity.
But that isn't always feasible. A great idea is to get
the already made pizza crust and any topping you
want. Let everybody get into the kitchen together
and make their very own style and flavor of pizza.
Everybody gets what they want and it is really fun
to do this all together.

Directions:

Pre-heat oven to 400 degrees F. Take pizza
crust and layer toppings with sauce, cheese,
meat, vegetables, or whatever else you can
think of. Bake on baking sheet for about 10
minutes, or until cooked thoroughly.

Tip:

Don't be afraid to experiment with different
combinations. Use gourmet cheese to add a
distinct flair to your pizza. Use anything from
gourmet toppings to whatever you have in
your pantry.

Burrito Bowl with Spaghetti Squash

Owner: Anna & Collin

Servings: 4-6

Prep Time: 1 hour

Total Time: 1 hour and 30 minutes

Ingredients:

1 spaghetti squash
4 chicken breasts, cut into long strips
1 can diced tomatoes, with Mexican spices
1 can black beans or refried beans
2 packets fajita seasoning
1/2 medium red onion, cut into large slices
1/2 medium green pepper, cut into large slices
1 avocado, cubed (optional)
Shredded cheese (optional)
2 tablespoons olive oil
Salt and pepper

Directions:

Preheat oven to 350 degrees F. Cut squash in half (cutting through the long side of the squash). Remove seeds. Place both halves cut side down on baking sheet. Bake for 45 minutes. Let squash cool for about 15 minutes. Using a fork, scrap out the squash from the skin and place in bowl. (The squash will actually look like spaghetti noodles when it's scraped out.) Season with 1 packet of fajita seasoning. Set aside.

Place olive oil and chicken in large skillet. Cook for 5-10 minutes. Add onion, green pepper and cook for 5 minutes. Add additional olive oil if necessary to prevent sticking. Season with salt and pepper. Add diced tomatoes and cook until chicken is thoroughly cooked.

Heat beans according to can instructions. In large bowls, add beans, spaghetti squash, chicken and vegetable mixture. Top with avocado (optional) and shredded cheese.

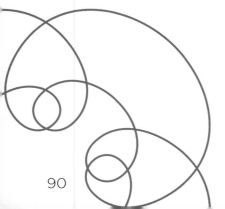

Sam's Fried Rosemary Chicken Strips

Owner: Sam
Servings: 4
Prep Time: 20
Total Time: 30 minutes

Ingredients:

4 chicken breasts, with fat trimmed and
cut into strips
2 cups flour
1 cup buttermilk
1 cup cornmeal
1 teaspoon red pepper flakes
1 tablespoon cayenne pepper
1/2 cup fresh rosemary, crushed or finely
chopped
1/2 - 1 cup vegetable oil, enough to cover
bottom of pan up to about 1/2 inch
Paper bag, like a grocery sack

Directions:

First you'll need to take out the chicken and cut all the fat off. Then, place flour, cornmeal and spices (cayenne pepper, red pepper flakes and crushed rosemary) into paper bag.   Place 1 cup buttermilk into a bowl.   Dip the chicken strips in the buttermilk and then into the bag and shake to coat chicken.   Repeat for each strip dipping in buttermilk and flour mixture.   It is very important to coat them each twice. Put oil in large skillet and bring it to medium-high heat. Cook chicken strips in oil about 10 minutes on each side or until each side is golden brown and center is done.

Side Dish

Don's Incentive Shake

Owner: Don   **Servings:** 1 brave person with a tough stomach

Ingredients:

Whatever is on the table

Story:

When the kids were little, there was always the challenge to get them to eat a good dinner. One night I told the kids that if they ate their food, then they could make me a "shake" that had anything from the table in it. So if that night we were eating meatloaf or peas or cottage cheese, any of that stuff would go in a "shake". Pepper, salt, ketchup, whatever. The kids got so excited they immediately began to eat...and eat well. I remember looking at Sandi with that, "what have I gotten myself into" look.

Sure enough, the kids finished eating and took my water glass and began to put all kinds of stuff in that drink. And true to my word, I drank it. Well, not all of it. That wasn't the deal. Just drink some of it. Then I confessed to the kids that I used to make money in college doing this exact thing. In the cafeteria, other kids would dare me to drink the "shake." One semester I even made enough to pay for my books.

So, this may not be a recipe you'd like to "make," but you could seriously impress your kids by doing it and they'll clean their plates in the process.

-Don

Corn Casserole

Owner: Sandi
Servings: 8-10
Prep Time: 10 minutes
Total Time: 45 minutes to 1 hour

Ingredients:

1 can whole kernel corn, drained
1 can creamed corn
2 eggs, beaten
1 box Jiffy corn muffin mix
1 stick butter, melted (or 1/2 cup oil)
1 cup reduced fat sour cream
1/4-1/2 teaspoon garlic powder (optional)
Shredded Swiss cheese (optional)

Directions:

Preheat oven to 350 degrees F. Mix all ingredients (except for the cheese). Place ingredients into 9 x 13 non-stick prepared dish. Cook for about 40 minutes, remove from oven and add the Swiss cheese on top. Cook another 10-20 min or until cheese is melted and starting to brown.

Tip:

All of my family doesn't like the Swiss cheese so I add cheese to half of the casserole. Happiness is my goal.

Hot Potato Casserole

Owner: Betty Fair (long time friend and nanny of the kids)
Servings: 15
Prep Time: 20 minutes
Total Time: 50 minutes

Ingredients:

8-10 medium potatoes, with skin
1/2 pound Velveeta cheese, cubed
1/2 pint mayonnaise
1/2 cup onions, minced
1/2 cup black olives, sliced
1/2 cup bacon, cooked and crumbled
Salt and pepper, to taste

Directions:

Preheat oven to 350 degrees F.

Boil the potatoes until almost fork tender. Let them cool. Peel and dice into 1/2 inch cubes and place into large greased casserole dish.

Add the cheese, mayonnaise, onion, and salt & pepper into the casserole dish. Toss together to combine. Top with olives and bacon.

Bake, covered, for 15-20 minutes. Uncover and bake for the remaining 10 minutes.

Rice Pilaf

Owner: Sandi
Servings: 5-7
Prep Time: 20 minutes
Total Time: 40 minutes

Ingredients:

2 tablespoon oil
1/2 cup angel hair pasta broken
into small 1-1 1/2 inch pieces
2 cups water (or 2 cups chicken broth)
1/4 stick butter
4 chicken bouillon cubes (omit if using broth)
1/2 cup fresh parsley, finely chopped
1 cup long cooking rice

Directions:

Put oil into pan over med-high heat. When oil is hot, add the angel hair pasta pieces. Let pasta begin to brown (this will sneak up on you so watch them). Immediately, but slowly, add water. Add rice, butter, parsley and bouillon cubes. Turn heat down to low and cover. Let cook for 20-30 minutes until rice is done. Check and stir often.

Broccoli Casserole

Owner: Natalie (Sandi's Business Manager)
Servings: 8–12
Prep Time: 15 minutes
Total Time: 45 minutes

Ingredients:

Ingredients:
3 heads of broccoli
1 large cube of processed cheese, cut into slices
1 box butter wheat crackers
1 stick butter
2 tablespoons sugar
1 tablespoon salt
1/4 tablespoon pepper

Directions:

Fill pot with 1-inch of water. Add broccoli florets to water. Season broccoli with sugar, salt & pepper. Steam broccoli for 7-10 minutes. Drain broccoli and let completely cool. In a 9x13 pan layer cooled broccoli, slices of cheese, and crushed crackers. Melt butter and drizzle over crushed crackers.

Bake for 45 minutes uncovered at 350 degrees F

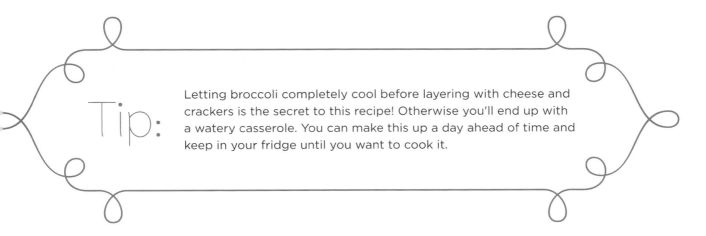

Tip: Letting broccoli completely cool before layering with cheese and crackers is the secret to this recipe! Otherwise you'll end up with a watery casserole. You can make this up a day ahead of time and keep in your fridge until you want to cook it.

Papa's Cornbread

Owner: Papa (Ron Patty-Sandi's dad)
Servings: 12
Prep Time: 20 minutes
Total Time: 40 minutes

. . . .

Ingredients:

1 cup yellow corn meal
1 cup flour
1 pinch of regular salt
1/4 of a cup sugar
1 teaspoon garlic salt
3/4 cup buttermilk
1/4 cup homogenized milk
1 beaten egg
1/3 hot melted butter (a little less than 3/4 of butter cup)

For Mexican Cornbread:
1/2 cup each of diced red, green and yellow peppers
1 diced jalapeño pepper
1/2 cup of diced onions
3 tablespoons of the salsa of your choice

Directions:

While mixing the ingredients, generously spread shortening in the muffin spaces. Preheat the oven to 425 degrees F and place the muffin pan in the oven, allowing the shortening to get smoking hot. Doing this allows the cornbread mixture to begin crusting the second it hits the hot shortening. At the same time, place the butter into a small bowl and heat in the microwave until it, too, gets boiling hot. Doing this will make the batter begin cooking from inside the second the butter is mixed in.

In a medium bowl, stir in the dry ingredients (corn meal, flour, garlic salt, salt, sugar and baking powder). Then stir in the buttermilk, homogenized milk and beaten egg. Take the hot butter from the microwave and mix it into the mixture. Take the hot muffin pan from the oven and fill each space liberally or with restraint (depending on how much crunch you want). Bake for 15-18 minutes, again depending on how brown you want the top.

For Mexican Cornbread, stir in the above ingredients before the hot butter is mixed in.

Story:

You may wind down in the evening with a nice cup of tea, or a piece of chocolate, or a bowl of cereal. But, my dad, Ron-more affectionately known as Papa-winds down with cornbread in a glass of cold milk. He lets the milk get all soaked up by the bread and eats it with a spoon. I thought it was the oddest thing when I was younger. But, now I absolutely love it. Try it. You might be surprised how much you like it.

- Sandi

Amazing Summer Slush

Owner: Sandi
Servings: 15-20
Prep Time: 15 minutes
Total Time: 15 minutes (freeze for 3 hours)

Ingredients:

3 cups water
5 bananas, sliced
1 6-ounce can frozen orange juice
1 8-ounce can unsweetened crushed pineapple
3 orange juice cans of water
1 6-ounce jar maraschino cherries cut in half

Directions:

Combine all ingredients and mix well in large bowl. Spoon out portion into 6-ounce clear plastic cups. Place cups in refrigerator for at least 3 hours or until firm. Before serving, allow mixture to thaw where it becomes "slushy."

Tip:

This is FANTASTIC on a hot day. Some people add sugar to this recipe but personally I don't think it needs it and I love the addition of the cherries. They will sink to the bottom so be sure to mix well before you eat it.

Skinny Green Beans

Owner: Sandi
Servings: 6-8
Prep Time: 5 minutes
Total Time: 20 minutes

. . . .

Ingredients:

3 cans green beans (not cut)
2-3 teaspoons beef bouillon

Directions:

Place beans with liquid, and bouillon in saucepan. Cover and let cook over medium heat for 15-20 min.
Drain and serve.

Tip:

The bouillon makes the beans taste like they have butter and bacon in it, without all of the calories. Fantastic trick for an easy side dish.

Refrigerator Slaw

Owner: Mike & Debbie Atkins (Sandi's Manager)
Servings:
Prep Time: 30 minutes
Total Time: 24 hours (Refrigerate overnight. 1 hour active cooking time.)

. . . .

Ingredients:

1 head cabbage, cut fine or grated
1 teaspoon salt
1 red pepper, cut fine
1 green pepper, cut fine
3 stalks celery, cut fine
1/2 teaspoon celery seed
1/2 teaspoon mustard seed
1 1/2 cups sugar
1 cup vinegar
1/2 cup water

Directions:

Mix cabbage and salt. Let stand 1 hour then squeeze water out. Mix with red pepper, green pepper, celery, celery seed and mustard seed. Boil together for 3 minutes, cool and pour over all ingredients. Cover and let stand overnight, will keep a week or more.

Cheesy Grits with Bacon

Owner: Anna & Collin
Servings: 5-6
Prep Time: 15 minutes
Total Time: 30 minutes

Ingredients:

2 cups water
1/2 cup instant grits
2 tablespoons butter or margarine
4 turkey bacon strips, baked and
cut into pieces
1/4 cup green onions, diced
1 teaspoon garlic salt
1 teaspoon kosher salt
1 teaspoon black pepper
5 ounces gouda cheese, shredded

Directions:

Set oven at 400 degrees F. Bake bacon strips in oven for 10 minutes, or until crispy. Cool slightly. Cut bacon strips into pieces. Set aside. In a medium saucepan, bring water to a boil. Stir in grits; reduce heat to medium-low. Stir grits for 3 minutes. Add butter. After butter is mixed in, add gouda. After gouda cheese is mixed in, add remaining ingredients. Stir in completely and reduce heat to low. Let grits thicken for 2 more minutes and serve.

Tip:

Grits go with a lot more than you think. Turn on many popular cooking TV shows and you'll see that grits are used in savory combinations with quite fancy ingredients. This recipe goes great with BBQ Shrimp (recipe on page 81). Shrimp and grits has long been a southern food staple. But if shellfish isn't your thing, try it with some spicy chicken or smoked sausage and a little sautéed onions. Play around with this grits recipe and make it your own.

Green Beans Casserole

Owner: Betty Fair (long time friend and nanny of the kids)
Servings: 8
Prep Time: 5 minutes
Total Time: 45 minutes

Ingredients:

3 cans green beans, drained (save 1 can liquid)
2 cans cream of mushroom soup
1 can water chestnuts, drained and sliced
1 medium onion, chopped
Salt and pepper
1 can fried onion rings

Directions

Preheat oven to 400 degrees F.
Place green beans in casserole dish and add remaining ingredients. Lightly mix together, until ingredients are incorporated.

Bake for 40 minutes. Add onions rings to top and continue baking for 5 minutes.

Sweet Potato Casserole

Owner: Betty Fair (long time friend and nanny of the kids)
Servings: 10
Prep Time: 10 minutes
Total Time: 50 minutes

Ingredients:

Potato Mixture:
1 large can sweet potatoes
1 cup brown sugar
2 eggs
1 stick margarine

Topping:
1 cup brown sugar
1 cup pecans
1/3 cup flour
1 stick margarine

Directions:

Preheat oven to 350 degrees F.

For Potato Mixture:
Whip ingredients (except those for topping) together in large bowl and pour mixture into greased 9x11 casserole dish.

For Topping:
Melt butter. Add remaining ingredients to butter. Spoon onto potato mixture and spread as evenly as possible
Baked, uncovered, for 30-40 minutes.

Sweet Potato Skinny Fries

Owner: Mollie
Servings: 8-10
Prep Time: 20 minutes
Total Time: 50 minutes

Ingredients:

5 sweet potatoes
3 tablespoons Parmesan cheese
1 tablespoon garlic powder
2 teaspoons salt
2 teaspoons finely chopped parsley
1 teaspoon pepper
Enough extra virgin olive oil to lightly coat the fries

Directions:

Preheat oven to 425 degrees F. Cut your fries so that they are 1/4 inch thick. It is important to cut them the same size so that the cooking time will be the same. In a small bowl add the seasonings, cheese, and parsley. Mix together and set aside. Place the cut fries into a large bowl and drizzle with oil. Use your fingers to move them around and make sure they are well coated. Pour the seasoning mix over the fries and make sure they are evenly coated. Place fries in a single layer on a cookie sheet. Make sure they are not touching and bake for 15 minutes. Turn the fries over and continue baking another 15 minutes. Let cool for a few minutes and then enjoy!

Tip:

Serve with chipotle aioli from Fish Taco recipe on page 77.

Don's Christmas Mashed Potatoes

Owner: Don

Servings: An unsuspecting table of relatives

Story:

It was in the early 1970's and I must have been 9-10 years old at this particular Christmas Holiday gathering. Our Peslis family holidays, for as long as I can remember, were held at our house. The house was decorated and full of relatives-a scene right out of "My Big Fat Greek Wedding"-and everyone was sitting down at the dining room table to begin the traditional Christmas feast. Of course, what I really meant to say was that the adults were in the dining room and my cousin Chris and I were seated at the kitchen table. This wasn't a bad thing because Chris and I had a bird's eye view of all the food as it went from stovetop to our table just before it went out to the dining room for the feast. My mother just happened to set a piping hot bowl of mashed potatoes in front of me.

Well, in keeping with good cousin tradition, there was always laughter, fun, and good times and this gathering was no exception. Chris had just shared something incredibly funny and at the same time I took a generous drink of red fruit juice. What he shared I still can't remember to this day. However, what happened next is forever ingrained in both our minds. As my mom turned back to the stove, out of both of my nostrils came, in jet-like fashion, bright red juice right into the piping hot bowl of mashed potatoes.

Time stood still.

I looked at Chris with eyes wide and gaping, then looked at the now piping-hot bowl of mashed potatoes seemingly sprinkled with Christmas delight. What was I to do? I quickly took the spoon and began to cover my red tracks with many heaping spoonfuls of mashed potatoes that I had pulled up from the bottom of the bowl. Without missing a beat my mother, who was totally unaware of all that had just transpired in the past five seconds, takes the piping hot bowl of mashed potatoes to my awaiting and unsuspecting family. Chris' face was still frozen. But when my mom passed into the other room we erupted in laughter. To this day it remains one of our greatest Christmas holiday legends.

-Don

Roasted Vegetables

Owner: Sandi
Servings: 8-10
Prep Time: 15 minutes
Total Time: 45 minutes

Ingredients:

1 summer squash
1 zucchini
5-6 red potatoes
4-5 carrots
1 stalk broccoli (cut into small pieces)
1 stalk cauliflower (cut into small pieces)
2 cups sliced mushrooms
1 cup whole fresh green beans
8 small chunks of corn on the cob
1 medium red onion (cut into 2-inch pieces)
1/2 cup olive oil
Salt and pepper to taste (make sure to do an even sprinkle over all of the vegetables)
1/2 cup parmesan cheese

Directions:

Preheat oven at 400 degrees F. In a large roasting pan, put in cut up fresh vegetables. Drizzle vegetables with olive oil. Roast in oven for about 20-30 minutes. Sprinkle with parmesan cheese and serve.

Tip:

This is one of our favorite foods to have in the summer. Great time for fresh vegetables and it's so easy. This goes great with some simple chicken fresh from the grill.

Old Fashioned Mac & Cheese with Ham

Owner: Betty Fair (long time friend and nanny of the kids)
Servings: 6-8
Prep Time: 15 minutes
Total Time: 1 hour

Ingredients:

7 ounce package macaroni, cooked and drained
1 pound cooked ham, finely diced
1 pound shredded cheddar cheese
1 cup onion, minced (optional)
12 ounce can low fat evaporated milk, undiluted
Salt and pepper

Directions:

Grease 9x13 baking dish and Preheat oven to 375 degrees F.

In large bowl, mix cooked macaroni, ham, minced onion (optional), cheese, salt and pepper. Spoon into baking dish. Pour milk evenly over ingredients. Bake for 45 minutes or until top is slightly golden brown.

Desserts

"Baseball Cake" or "Tunnel Fudge Cake"

Owner: Nana (Carolyn Patty-Sandi's Mom)
Servings: 10-12
Prep Time: 15 minutes
Total Time: 1 hour 15 minutes

Ingredients:

1/2 cup margarine
6 eggs
1 1/2 cup sugar
2 cups sifted flour
1 package fudge chocolate icing mix
2 cups chopped walnuts

Directions:

Preheat oven to 350 degrees F. Cream the margarine in a bowl with an electric mixer. Add in the eggs one at a time, waiting between each addition to make sure it is incorporated. Add in sugar and continue to mix by hand. Add in the flour, icing mix, and walnuts. Mix well and pour into the bundt pan. Bake for 1 hour. Cool cake in bundt pan for 1-2 hours. Release cake by turning over bundt pan onto plate.

Make sure cake is cooled completely before covering.

Story:

The reason we started calling this fantastic cake a baseball cake is because it is made in a Bundt pan. One day, when we were all over at Nana and Papa's house for a holiday get together, Anna's husband, Collin saw this cake that Nana had made on the counter. Collin said to Nana, "This looks amazing. What is that pan called?" Nana told him the cake was made in a Bundt pan. Collin said, "Oh, it's a baseball cake." (Get it? Because you bunt in baseball.) From then on it has forever been call Nana's baseball cake.

- Sandi

Banana Cake ("Oleta Cake")

Recipe on following page.

Story:

Betty Fair has been a part of our family for many years. I knew Betty and her husband Phil when I was in college at Anderson University and would often go over to their house to escape from the dorm life. When Anna was a baby, Betty started working for us as a nanny and helped us raise all 8 of our kids. To say that she is a fixture in our lives would be an understatement. We adore Betty.

She has retired from the nanny world in the past few years but she remains every close to our hearts. In fact, she and Phil now live in Oklahoma City (as do we) and we live just around the corner from each other.

Betty grew up in an Armenian family—in fact, Betty's mother and father came over to America through Ellis Island when there were both young. Betty is a first generation here in America. Again, like Don's Greek family, Armenian families are all about food, dinners, family connection and hospitality.

Our kids always loved when Betty would cook because there were so many fantastic things she would make. One of the favorite things Betty would make is something we call Oleta Cake. It's really a banana cake, but many years ago Betty got this recipe from someone named Oleta (O-lee-tah) and it has gone by that name ever since.

We would usually do grocery shopping at the beginning of the week and by Friday the bananas would be looking a little dark. The kids would then begin to murmur amongst themselves, "oh yeah the bananas are bad. It's time for Betty to make Oleta Cake." And so she did and would leave one on the stove for us to enjoy during the weekend.

One last little tidbit about this Oleta Cake. For years, Betty made this cake with no icing because she never realized there was icing. The truth is, in all these years, she never turned the recipe card over to read the directions for the icing. Betty made this discovery only a few years ago and we have laughed about it since.

I will include the directions for icing, although we've never had it, and I'm not sure I would even like it with icing after all these years, but nevertheless here it is.

- Sandi

Oleta Cake (Banana)

Owner: Betty
Servings: 10-12
Prep Time: 15 minutes
Total Time: 55 minutes

Ingredients:

2/3 cup shortening
1 1/2 cup sugar
2 eggs
2 cups flour
1 teaspoon baking soda
1/2 teaspoon salt
1/2 cup buttermilk
1 teaspoon vanilla
1 teaspoon lemon juice
1/2 cup nuts (optional)
2-3 bananas

Directions:

Grease and flour a 11x13 pan and preheat oven to 325 degrees F.

Cream together the shortening and sugar. Add the eggs into mixture. Mix until incorporated.

In a small bowl, add the flour, soda and salt. Mix well. Add the flour mixture to the egg and sugar mixture. Add the remaining ingredients and mix well. Pour mixture into prepared pan.

Bake 35-40 minutes

Oleta Cake Icing :

8 ounce package cream cheese
1 stick softened butter or margarine
1 16-ounce box confectioners Sugar-sifted
1 cup nuts, chopped (if desired)
1/2 teaspoon black walnut flavoring
1/4 cup coconut (if desired)

Cream together cream cheese and butter or margarine. Mix in remaining ingredients. Spread onto cooled Oleta Cake.

Mike Patty's Turtle Cake

Owner: Mike (Sandi's Brother)
Servings: 8-12
Prep Time: 30 minutes
Total Time: 52 minutes

Ingredients:

For Caramel:

14 ounce caramel
1/2 cup margarine, softened
1/2 cup evaporated milk

For Cake

1 box German chocolate cake mix
1/2 cup evaporated milk
3/4 cup margarine
1 cup pecans
1 cup chocolate chips

Directions:

For Caramel:

Mix together all ingredients and soften in microwave. Set aside.

For Cake:

Grease 9x13 pan and preheat oven to 350 degrees F. Mix together and divide in two. (The mixture may be a bit stiff. Make sure to mix well.)

Spoon half of mixture into cake pan. Bake for 7 minutes. Remove cake from oven and pour the caramel mixture over the cake. Sprinkle pecans and chocolate chips over cake. Spread remaining cake batter on top. Bake another 15 minutes. Set aside to cool to room temperature.

Tip:

Make sure to use a bag of raspberries, as the boxed raspberries have way too much juice and ruin the consistency of the cake and frosting. If you don't have any gelatin, I have omitted the gelatin and just added 3 tablespoons of flour instead of 1 tablespoon. I have also made this recipe with fresh raspberries, using 1 cup for both the frosting and the cake.

Gloria Gaither's Red Raspberry Cake

Owner: Gloria Gaither (Friend of Sandi)
Servings: 8-10
Prep Time: 20 minutes
Total Time: 45-55 minutes

Ingredients:

Cake:
1 box white cake mix
1 small box raspberry gelatin mixture
1 tablespoon flour
4 eggs
1 cup water
1/3 cup oil
1/2 bag frozen raspberries

Frosting:
1 stick of butter
1 box powdered sugar, about 1.5 pounds
1/2 bag frozen raspberries

Directions:

Cake:
Preheat oven at 350 degrees F. Mix the white cake mix, box of raspberry gelatin, and flour together. Add the eggs, water, oil and frozen raspberries. Mix well and divide mix between 3 eight-inch pans, which have been greased and floured. Bake for 20-25 minutes. Cool cake completely.

Frosting:
Cream butter with electric mixer. Gradually mix in powdered sugar. Stir in raspberries by hand. (Frosting needs to be somewhat thick so feel free to add more powdered sugar.) Frost cake once it is completely cooled. Place frosting on first layer, stack next layer and repeat. Frost cake around base and top.

Story:

Gloria Gaither has been a friend and mentor for many years. The funny thing about this cake is that Gloria has never made it personally for us but one time I was doing the Joni Lamb television show and Joni wanted me to help her cook that day on the show. She introduced me to Gloria's magnificent Red Raspberry Cake. And our family has loved it ever since. I am a huge fan of chocolate for dessert and rarely ever stray far from a chocolate cake. However if anything can make me stray it is Gloria's Red Raspberry Cake. The color is a beautiful bright pink and it is delicious! This will surely impress any guests. Enjoy!

 - Sandi

Apple Pie

Owner: Aly
Servings: 8
Prep Time: 1 hour
Total Time: 2 hours

. . . .

Ingredients:

Pie Crust:
6 ounces cold unsalted butter
2 ounces vegetable shortening
5-7 tablespoons ice water (I also love to use apple cider in place of this if I have it)
2 3/4 cups all-purpose flour (have some extra out for dusting)
1 teaspoon salt
1 tablespoon sugar

Pie Filling:
3 pounds apples (I usually use 4 granny smith and 2 golden delicious)
1/4 cup white sugar
2 tablespoons brown sugar
1 1/2 teaspoon cinnamon
2 teaspoons corn starch
2 tablespoons lemon juice
1 tablespoon orange juice

Directions:

Pie Crust:
Butter and shortening should be cut into half inch pieces before baking process starts.
Make sure that these items along with the apple cider are cold.

In a bowl, combine the flour, salt and sugar. Using a fork; mix until just combined. Add the butter and mix until texture is crumbly. Add the shortening and combine.
Add in the apple cider a few tablespoons at a time until the mixture holds up and can be squeezed.
Divide the dough in half, roll into disks and wrap in plastic. Refrigerate.

Pie Filing:
Preheat oven to 425 degrees F. Peel and slice apples into 1/4 inch slices. Toss apples in sugars, cinnamon, lemon and orange juice. Place in colander with bowl underneath and let sit for 10 minutes. Take juice from apple mixture and mix in corn starch. Mix juice back in with apples.

Place piecrust in bottom of pie pan. Use a fork to poke a few holds in the bottom. Pour in pie filling. Cover with second piecrust.

You will want to make a few slits in the top of the piecrust, and brush it with an egg wash (1 egg mixed with 1 tablespoon ice water). Then dust with sugar.

Place pie on baking sheet to prevent leaking in the stove. Bake for 15 minutes and take pie out of oven. Line the outer edge of crust with a ring of foil. This will prevent the edges from burning. Place back in oven for another 35 minutes.
Ovens vary and so do pies. You may need less time, or you may need more. Just watch it!

Banana Pudding

Owner: Betty Fair (longtime friend and nanny of the children)
Servings: 8-10
Prep Time: 15 minutes
Total Time: 25 minutes

. . . .

Ingredients:

1 can sweetened condensed milk
1 1/2 cup water
1 package dry instant vanilla pudding
2 cups whipped cream, plus more for topping
1 box vanilla wafers
3 bananas, sliced

Directions:

Mix together sweetened condensed milk and water. Add in the pudding mix.
Mix well until there are no lumps. Fold in 2 cups of whipped cream.

Layer in serving bowl starting with pudding and continuing with wafers and bananas. There should be 3-5 layers. Continue until everything is used. Top with additional whipped cream. Chill and serve.

No Bake Cookies

Owner: Sandi
Servings: 1-2 dozen
Prep Time: 15 minutes
Total Time: 1 hour 15 minutes

. . . .

Ingredients:

2 cups sugar
1/4 cup cocoa
1/2 cup milk
1/4 pound margarine
1 teaspoon vanilla
1/2 cup chunky peanut butter
3 cups quick-cook oatmeal
Pinch salt

Directions:

Mix together sugar, cocoa, milk and margarine. Put in saucepan over medium heat and cook to a boil. Remove from heat and let set for 1 minute. Add the vanilla, salt, peanut butter, and oatmeal. Drop by the spoonful (whatever size you choose) on wax paper, and let cool in refrigerator.

Colossal Cookies

Owner: Carol Cutler (friend of the family)
Servings: 37 cookies
Prep Time: 10 minutes
Total Time: 22 minutes

Ingredients:

1/2 cup softened butter
1 1/2 cups granulated sugar
1 1/2 cups brown sugar
4 eggs
1 teaspoon vanilla
2 cups chunky peanut butter

1 18-ounce package of old-fashioned uncooked oats
1 cup chocolate chips
2 1/2 teaspoon soda

Directions:

Preheat oven to 350 degrees F. Cream together butter, granulated sugar and brown sugar. Mix well and add eggs, vanilla, chunky peanut butter. Stir in old-fashioned oats, chocolate chips, and soda. This is very thick and takes some strength to stir. Place 1/4 cup mixture on ungreased cookie sheet and flatten with a spatula. Place about 2 inches apart. (The cookies will enlarge to about 4 inches.) Bake 15 minutes. Cool a minute or two before moving or they will brake.

To freeze cookie dough:
Measure 1/4 cup dough and place each on a cookie sheet. Don't flatten. Freeze until firm and store in a plastic bag. When ready to bake, thaw for about 30 minutes on the cookie sheet before cooking as directed. Makes about 37 colossal cookies.

Story:

My parents have been friends with a couple, Ken and Carol Cutler, for more years than I have been born. They met each other in Oklahoma City in 1956 at the church my dad was minister of music, Shartel Church of God. My mom was pregnant with me so there has not been a day in my life when I have not known Carol and Ken. They have been like second parents to me. Papa Ken passed away a few years ago and we miss him so much. "Grandma" Carol lives in Oklahoma City and I have so loved being back in her life on a personal, live-by-you kind of way. She is a fabulous cook. In fact the meatloaf that is my favorite is her recipe. These are my favorite cookies that she makes and so with her blessing I share them with you. Be prepared—they are addicting.

- Sandi

Pumpkin Snickerdoodles

Owner: Jenn
Servings: 36
Prep Time: 20 minutes
Total Time: 40-70 minutes

Ingredients:

2 1/2 cups all-purpose flour
1 teaspoon baking powder
1 teaspoon baking soda
3-4 teaspoons pumpkin pie spice
1/2 teaspoon salt
1/2 cup unsalted butter, softened
1 cup canned pumpkin
1 egg
1 cup brown sugar
1/2 cup white sugar
1 teaspoon vanilla extract
2 tablespoons white sugar
2 teaspoons ground cinnamon

Directions:

Preheat oven to 350 degrees F. Whisk flour, baking powder, baking soda, pumpkin pie spice, and salt in a medium bowl. Set aside. Cream butter and brown and white sugar in a large bowl. Beat pumpkin, egg, and vanilla into creamed butter and sugar, and mix until creamy. With a wooden spoon, mix the dry ingredients into the wet until just blended.
Refrigerate dough for at least 30 minutes (not necessary, but the chilled dough will make rolling the cookies much easier). Mix cinnamon and sugar in a small bowl. Roll tablespoons of dough in the cinnamon sugar mixture and place on cookie sheets lined with parchment paper. Bake 15-20 minutes. Cool on wire racks.

Five Minute Fudge

Owner: Nana (Sandi's Mom Carolyn)
Servings: 24
Prep Time: 10 minutes
Total Time: 45 minutes

Ingredients:

2/3 cups undiluted evaporated milk (skim or low fat)
1 2/3 cup sugar
1/3 teaspoon salt
1 1/2 cup mini marshmallows
1 1/2 cup chocolate chips
1/2 teaspoon vanilla
1/2 cup chopped walnuts (optional)

Directions:

Place the milk, sugar, and salt into a saucepan over medium heat. Stir until boiling and then boil for 5 minutes, stirring constantly. Remove from heat and add the marshmallows, chips, vanilla and walnuts (optional).
Stir until chocolate is melted and then pour into buttered 9-inch pan. Cool, then cut into squares and serve.

(Don't forget to lick the spoon!)

Hot Chocolate Mix

Owner: Betty Fair (long time friend and nanny of the kids)
Servings: 3 quarts of mix

Ingredients:

2 quarts powdered milk
1 small container cocoa powder
1 cup powdered sugar
1 cup sugar
11 ounces powdered coffee creamer

Directions:

Mix together ingredients and store in air tight container.

For Hot Chocolate:
Fill at least 1/2 of mug with dry mixture and add boiling water. Stir and enjoy.
Top with marshmallows.

Nana's Chocolate Peanut Butter Fudge

Owner: Nana (Carolyn Patty, Sandi's mom)
Servings: 20 pieces of fudge
Prep Time: 45
Total Time: 2-3 hours

· ·

Ingredients:

3 cups granulated sugar
5 tablespoons Hershey's cocoa
1 1/2 cup vitamin D milk
1 teaspoon vanilla
1/2 stick butter
4 heaping tablespoons crunchy
peanut butter

Story:

Let me just say this about Nana's
fudge. It does take a while and
you have to stay at it. You have to
stir it a lot. But, I'm just saying it's
worth it and it freezes really well.
So you can make a bunch ahead
of time and save it for later. It is
magnificent. Trust me!

- Sandi

Directions:

Use a larger than medium metal pot. Mix sugar, milk and cocoa
over medium heat. With a metal spoon, stir frequently. Bring
to a boil, than turn down heat a little. After fudge continues
at a boil for 10-15 minutes (stirring periodically), begin testing
consistency by dropping a little of the fudge into a small glass
cup of water. With right index finger, swirl the fudge droplet
(you'll need to make several trial runs) until it forms a firm, yet
still soft ball. While the mixture is cooking, measure out the
butter, peanut butter, and vanilla. Also, pour two inches of cool
water in a sink with a stopper. When the ball mentioned above
is firm enough, set a large square glass pan in the sink water.
Then, put in the butter, vanilla and peanut butter in the pot on
the stove. Do not stir. Set the timer for 10 minutes. Prepare the
pan that will eventually hold the finished fudge by coating it
with a light coat of stick butter (not melted butter). When the
timer goes off, with the pan still in the cool water, use a wooden
spoon to begin stirring the pot with all of the ingredients. Keep
stirring until mixture thickens somewhat and loses some of
its sheen, taking on a dull-like appearance. Quickly pour the
mixture into the buttered-prepared pan. Let cool until fudge
hardens enough to cut into pieces.

Tip:

Keep in mind: If the ball of fudge mentioned above is not firm enough, then the stirring will take longer and may not harden (except for hot fudge for ice cream). If the ball is just right or too hard and you stir too long the fudge will turn to sugar and will be too hard (except for easy-to-please grandchildren). Rain or even humid weather may affect the outcome.

Fruit Cocktail Cake

Owner: Betty (longtime friend and nanny of the children)
Servings: 10-12
Prep Time: 5 minutes
Total Time: 35 minutes

. . . .

Ingredients:

Cake:
1 1/2 cup white sugar
2 cups flour
2 teaspoons baking soda
1/4 teaspoon salt
2 eggs
2 cups fruit cocktail with juice

Topping:
3/4 cup white sugar
1/2 cup milk
1 stick butter or margarine
1 teaspoon vanilla
1 cup coconut (optional)

Directions:

For Cake:
Grease and flour cake pan and preheat oven to 350 degrees F. Combine all ingredients for cake and add to cake pan. Bake for 30 minutes.

For Topping:
In a saucepan, bring sugar, milk and butter to a boil. Cook for an additional 2 minutes. Remove from heat. Add in the vanilla and coconut. Stir and pour over hot cake.

Vanilla Married Raspberry Cake

Owner: Aly
Servings: 8-12
Prep Time: 30 minutes
Total Time: 1 hour and 30 minutes

. . . .

Tip:

This is a very delicate cake, so the batter should be separated into three equal parts. This is so there is no cutting to create the layers. This step will be much easier if you are using a scale. You will have three even 9 inch cake layers. If you do not have a scale, just do your best to eyeball it.

If you want to go really crazy, use the original measurements for the pastry cream and cover the cake in the chocolate ganache!

Ingredients:

Cake:

2 cups fine granulated sugar
1 cup butter
4 eggs
3 teaspoons vanilla extract
1 teaspoon almond extract (if you don't have almond you can just use 4 teaspoons vanilla)
3 cups all-purpose flour
3 1/2 teaspoons baking powder
1 cup milk
Dark chocolate bar (optional)
1 cup canned raspberry preserves

Also use pastry cream from Chocolate Butter Cake Explosion on page 132.

Directions:

Preheat oven to 350 degrees F and line the bottom of three round cake pans with parchment paper.

In a bowl, cream together the sugar and butter on low speed until smooth, about 3 minutes. Combine the flour and baking powder in another bowl. Wisk together for 10 seconds to combine and then set aside. Add in the eggs one at a time to sugar and butter mix, and wait between each addition until incorporated. Add in the flour mixture, mix, and then add the milk. Grate the chocolate into the batter until flakes are visible throughout. Divide batter and pour into prepared pans. Bake 30-40 minutes until cake is springs back after touch and a toothpick comes out clean. Let cool 15 minutes in pans, and then turn out on flat surface. Leave to finish cooling to room temperature. Wrap in plastic and refrigerate.

Make vanilla pastry cream (recipe on page 132), enough for 1 1/2 batches.

Layer the cake, pastry cream, your favorite raspberry preserves, and repeat until finished.
Use the remaining pastry cream to cover cake. This works best with cold cakes and cooled pastry cream. If you use the cream right out of the fridge then it will make the cake crumble.

Chocolate Tower

Owner: Ginger Richey (friend of Sandi's)
Servings: 8-10
Prep Time: 20-30 minutes
Total Time: 30-40 minutes

Ingredients:

1 box store bought chocolate brownie mix
2 packages instant chocolate mousse, prepared
8 large chocolate covered toffee bars, or 1
12-ounce bag of chocolate toffee bits
2 pints whipping cream, whipped,
1 teaspoon vanilla extract
1/2 cup powdered sugar
3 tablespoons of shaved chocolate

Directions:

Prepare box of brownies according to directions. Cut into 2-inch cubes and set aside. Prepare chocolate mousse according to box instructions. In a medium mixing bowl, add vanilla and powdered sugar to whipping cream and whip until light and fluffy. In a trifle bowl, layer half of the brownies, chocolate mousse, toffee bars and whipped cream. Repeat layers. End with whipped cream topping. Garnish with shaved chocolate. Keep refrigerated until ready to serve.

Story:

Ginger is one of my new dear friends in Oklahoma City. And girl, can she cook. This is my absolute favorite recipe she has made and I am so crazy about it, I eat way too much. It is awesome and so is my friend, Ginger.

- Sandi

Peanut Butter Balls

Owner: Don
Servings: 25
Prep Time: 15 minutes
Total Time: 2 hours

Ingredients:

1/2 cup peanut butter
1/2 cup honey
1 cup whole oats
1 cup instant dry milk

Directions:

Mix all ingredients together in large bowl. Form into large marble size balls. Place in refrigerator for about 2 hours or (this is what I do) place in freezer for about 15 min. These are best served chilled. After these have set in either the refrigerator or freezer, keep them in a zip-top bag in the refrigerator.

Story:

Don used to work in the public schools in Anderson, Indiana, with a program called "Healthy Kids." He and another first grade teacher started this program to help kids understand what it is to make some healthy choices both in eating and exercising. The first grade teacher, Judy Moore, would bring these incredible healthy snacks. This recipe has become one of our family's favorites and a healthy snack for me when I need something sweet.

– Sandi

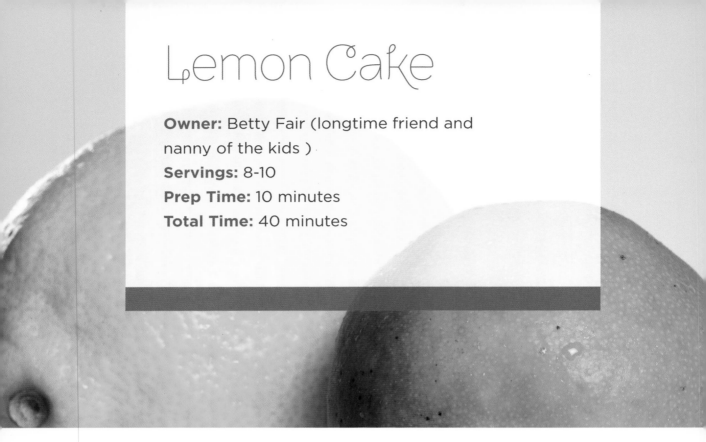

Lemon Cake

Owner: Betty Fair (longtime friend and nanny of the kids)
Servings: 8-10
Prep Time: 10 minutes
Total Time: 40 minutes

Ingredients:

Cake:

1 box moist lemon cake mix
1 small box lemon gelatin mix
3/4 cup canola oil
3/4 cup water
4 eggs

Topping:

1 1-pound box powdered sugar
6 tablespoons lemon juice

Directions:

Spray cake pan. (You can use whatever cake pan you have handy. Glass, metal, it all works.)

Preheat oven to 325 degrees F for glass pans or 350 degrees F for metal pans.

Mix all ingredients for cake together until combined. Pour into cake pan and bake for 25-30 minutes.

In the meantime, mix ingredients for topping in a small bowl and set aside.

When cake is done, poke holes in it with a fork. Pour Topping over cake. Do this as soon as it comes out of the oven. Let cool slightly before serving.

Cranberry Walnut Oatmeal Cookies

Owner: Jenn
Servings: 35
Prep Time: 36 minutes
Total Time: 35 minutes

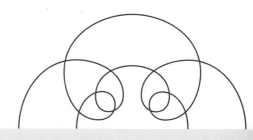

Ingredients:

1 cup orange juice
1/2 cup dried cranberries
1 cup unsalted butter, softened
1 cup packed light brown sugar
1/2 cup white sugar
2 eggs
1 teaspoon vanilla extract
3/4 cups whole wheat flour
3/4 cups all-purpose flour
2-3 teaspoons pumpkin pie spice
1/2 teaspoon salt
3 cups rolled oats
1/2 cup chopped walnuts
1/2 cup white chocolate chips

Directions:

Preheat oven to 350 degrees F.
Soak the cranberries in the orange juice for 30 minutes. Whisk the flours, baking soda, pumpkin pie spice, salt, and oats in a medium bowl. Set aside. Cream butter and sugars in a large bowl. Beat in eggs and vanilla until smooth. With a wooden spoon, mix dry ingredients into the wet until just blended. Drain the orange juice from the cranberries. Mix in cranberries, white chocolate chips, and walnuts into the batter, being careful not to over mix.

Roll tablespoons of dough and place onto cookie sheets lined with parchment paper. Bake 10 minutes. Cool on wire racks.

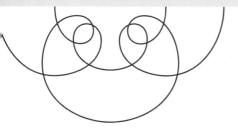

Chocolate Butter Cake Explosion

Owner: Aly
Servings: 8-12 cake servings or 24 cupcakes
Prep Time: 30 minutes
Total Time: 1 hour 15 minutes

Ingredients:

1 1/4 cups plus 2 tablespoons all purpose flour
1/2 cup unsweetened cocoa powder
1 and 1/2 teaspoons of baking powder
1 teaspoon salt
1 cup half and half
2 tablespoons apple juice
1 tablespoon pure vanilla extract
1 1/2 (6 ounces) sticks unsalted room temperature butter
1 3/4 cup fine granulated sugar
4 large eggs

Vanilla Pastry Cream:
Prep time 15 minutes Total time 30 minutes
2 1/2 cups whole milk
1 vanilla bean
6 large yolks
1 teaspoon vanilla extract
1/2 cup plus 3 tablespoons fine granulated sugar
5 tablespoons all-purpose flour

Chocolate Ganache:
1 1/2 cups 60% bittersweet chocolate disks (pistols)
1 cup heavy cream

Directions:

This recipe has quite a few steps. There are three separate parts to this entire cake. You have the Chocolate butter cake, the Filling Cream, and then finally the Chocolate Ganache.

Chocolate Cake:
Preheat oven to 350 degrees F and place the rack in the middle of the oven. Place dry ingredients in a bowl and whisk for 10 seconds and set aside. Put liquid ingredients in bowl and set aside. Place butter and sugar in a bowl (if using a stand mixer use the mixer bowl for this step). Crack the eggs and place them in a separate bowl.

Using the Paddle attachment on your mixer, cream the butter and sugar together on the lowest speed until light and fluffy. Keeping mixer on lowest speed, add eggs in one at a time. Wait until each egg is incorporated before adding the next. Scrape down the sides of the bowl. Start adding in the liquid and dry ingredients. You will want to alternate between the two; start with the dry and end with the dry. Move quickly so as not to over work the batter. Scrape down the sides and bottom of the bowl and turn mixer on medium speed for 15 seconds.

Line the bottom of each pan with parchment paper; do not spray the sides.

(If you are making cupcakes, once again do not spray the pan. The exception is spraying the top so that it is easier to take out the cupcakes.)

Bake 9-inch rounds for 28 minutes. (Bake cupcakes for 22 minutes.)
Cakes will be ready when a toothpick comes out clean. Let cool in the pan and turn out onto flat surface.
You can separate into layers at this point, and then wrap in cling plastic to refrigerate. Cake can be stored for a week in the fridge. (But, I doubt it will last that long with it being so delicious!)

Vanilla Pastry Cream
 Measure the milk into a heavy-bottom saucepan. Prepare the vanilla bean by slicing in half and then scraping out the seeds. Add seeds and pod to milk. Bring to boil over medium heat. Turn off heat and let sit for 10 minutes.

In a separate bowl combine the yolks, vanilla extract, sugar and flour. Wisk to combine.

Bring milk mixture back to a simmer, and then remove the pod. Add a small amount of milk mixture to yolks, about 2 tablespoons, and stir quickly. This tempers the mixture. Slowly add milk mixture to the yolk mixture. I mean slowly, or you will get a gross egg scramble thing. Wisk in small circles at first and then as you go you can stir slower until combined. Pour back into the saucepan. Heat over

medium heat, constantly whisking, for about 4 minutes. (There is no need to whisk rapidly. The ingredients are already mixed at this point. Whisking is only to make sure that the cream does not burn.) When you start to see lots of bubbles reduce to low and whisk briskly for 1 minute. Pour the cream into a shallow mixing bowl and cover with plastic wrap. Let the plastic touch the surface of the cream to prevent a skin from forming.

Chocolate Ganache
In a saucepan, bring the cream to a simmer. Place chocolate in a heat resistant bowl and once the cream is simmering, pour over chocolate. Let sit for 10 seconds so that the cream can distribute. Whisk to combine. Let the Ganache cool for about 8 minutes before using. It will melt pastry cream, or crumble the cake if it is too warm.

Assembly:
Place a layer of cake, and then 1 cup of pastry cream on top. Spread and then repeat. When you have all your layers; take the cooled ganache and spread over the cake.

Story:

This recipe has been adapted from several recipes I've used. I started making chocolate cake a long time ago, and watched people make them long before that. I have taken my favorite parts of recipes from my family, friends, favorite cookbooks, and my favorite blogs. I've changed up the ingredients and amounts and perfected it. Well, at least I've made my best version. What you have here is my favorite version... right now.

– Aly

Chocolate Sheet Cake

Owner: Sandi
Servings: 24
Prep Time: 15 minutes
Total Time: 1 hour

Ingredients:

Cake:

2 cups sugar
2 cups flour
1/4 teaspoons salt
2 cubes butter
4 tablespoons cocoa
1 cup water
1/2 cup buttermilk
2 eggs, well-beaten
1 teaspoon baking soda
1 teaspoon salt

Icing:

1 stick butter or margarine
4 tablespoons cocoa
6 tablespoons milk
3 1/2 cups powdered sugar

Directions:

Cake:

Mix together sugar, flour and salt in a bowl. Set aside. Preheat oven to 350 degrees F. Bring to boil butter, cocoa and water. Mix together all ingredients until well incorporated. Bake for 20 minutes in 11x13 pan. Let cake cool for about 20-30 minutes.

Icing:

Stir all ingredients and bring to light boil. Add powdered sugar and stir. Pour over cake and spread evenly. (You can also top the cake with 1 cup chopped pecans.)